Table of Contents

Management

Lessons

Unit I—Numbers and Counting

Table of Contents

Level
6–8

Getting to the Roots

of Mathematics Vocabulary

rotation
concentric
polygon

Authors

Timothy Rasinski, Ph.D.

Nancy Padak, Ed.D.

Rick M. Newton, Ph.D.

Evangeline Newton, Ph.D.

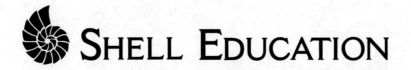

SHELL EDUCATION

Publishing Credits

Robin Erickson, *Production Director*; Lee Aucoin, *Creative Director*;
Timothy J. Bradley, *Illustration Manager*; Sara Johnson, M.S.Ed., *Editorial Director*;
Jennifer Viñas, *Editor*; Grace Alba, *Designer*; Corinne Burton, M.A.Ed., *Publisher*

Image Credits

p.23, Wikimedia Commons; All other images Shutterstock

Standards

© 2004 Mid-continent Research for Education and Learning (McREL)
© 2010 National Governors Association Center for Best Practices and Council of Chief State School Officers (CCSS)

Shell Education

5301 Oceanus Drive
Huntington Beach, CA 92649-1030
http://www.shelleducation.com
ISBN 978-1-4258-0866-2
© 2014 Shell Educational Publishing, Inc.

Mathematics Vocabulary Research and Practice

Words are labels for key concepts in mathematics. Although learning these words is critical to student success in math, teaching them can be challenging. Asking students to look words up in dictionaries or textbook glossaries and then to memorize definitions provides, at best, a short-term solution. Many mathematical ideas are new to students, and most of the concepts are abstract. Moreover, students may have insufficient background knowledge to learn these new concepts well, let alone to use them in computations.

> **Over 90 percent of all academic vocabulary (including mathematics) derives from Greek and Latin roots.**

In this book, we present a systematic, research-based, and engaging alternative to vocabulary memorization: a roots approach. First, we define our terms: a *root* is an umbrella term for "a word part or pattern that carries meaning." Since the human brain is programmed to detect patterns, a roots approach capitalizes on something that our brains do well. The three kinds of roots are prefixes, bases, and suffixes. Nearly every academic word consists of roots. This book presents 34 Greek and Latin word roots that generate hundreds of words.

Our understanding of a word's meaning begins not with the prefix but, rather, with the "base," because the base is the root that provides the core meaning. The bases that lie at the foundation of mathematical vocabulary are "basic" in that they express such essential and readily comprehensible ideas as numbers and counting, geometry, spatial relationships, and the metric system. This is why we say, "Bases are basic." When a student encounters a long mathematical word, a knowledge of roots enables him or her to "divide and conquer" it. The student is then able to identify the word's basic meaning, which might otherwise be confusing or overwhelming. A roots approach to vocabulary empowers students to look inside a long word and identify its roots that provide the keys to its meaning. Moreover, because roots are used in a great number of academic words, a roots approach is ideal for developing students' vocabulary in the various academic content areas. As students learn these word parts and recognize them as the essential components in specific words from math, their growing verbal skills support their increasing ability to comprehend math principles, as well as to increase and enhance their general vocabulary.

Mathematics Vocabulary Research and Practice (cont.)

What Does Research Say About Using a Roots Approach?

The size and depth of students' vocabulary is associated with proficiency in reading comprehension (Baumann et al. 2002; Beck, Perfetti, and McKeown 1982; Kame'enui, Carnine, and Freschi 1982; Stahl and Fairbanks 1986).

Morphological analysis (e.g., via a roots approach) is important because it is generative and allows students to make connections among semantically-related words or word families (Nagy and Scott 2000). Developing morphological awareness is an integral component of word learning (Biemiller and Slonim 2001). In a comprehensive review of 16 studies analyzing the effect of instruction in morphological awareness on literacy achievement, Carlisle (2010) observes that people learn morphemes as they learn language.

Classroom-based studies have demonstrated the effectiveness of teaching word parts and context clues in the primary and intermediate grades (Baumann et al. 2002; Baumann et al. 2005; Biemiller 2005; Carlisle 2000; Kieffer and Lesaux 2007; Mountain 2005; Porter-Collier 2010). Research in content-area vocabulary has demonstrated the effectiveness of teaching Greek and Latin word roots, especially for struggling readers (Harmon, Hedrick, and Wood 2005). Moreover, vocabulary knowledge is associated with higher scores on high-stakes tests like the ACT; students with knowledge of Latin score significantly higher on the SAT than those without such knowledge (ACT 2006; LaFleur 1981).

No single instructional method is sufficient. Teachers need a variety of methods that teach word meanings while also increasing the depth of word knowledge (Blachowicz et al. 2006; Lehr, Osborn, and Hiebert 2004). These methods should aim at fostering:

Immersion

Students need frequent opportunities to use new words in diverse oral and print contexts in order to learn them thoroughly (Blachowicz and Fisher 2006).

Metacognitive and metalinguistic awareness

Students must understand and know how to manipulate the structural features of language (Nagy and Scott 2000).

Word consciousness

Word exploration (e.g., etymology) and word play (e.g., puns, riddles, games) help students develop an awareness of and interest in words (Graves and Watts-Taffe 2002; Lehr, Osborn, and Hiebert 2004).

Mathematics Vocabulary Research and Practice *(cont.)*

Why Teach with a Roots Approach?

Teaching with a roots approach is efficient. Over 60 percent of the words students encounter in their reading have recognizable word parts (Nagy et al. 1989). Moreover, content-area vocabulary is largely of Greek and Latin origin (Harmon, Hedrick, and Wood 2005). Many words from Greek and Latin roots meet the criteria for "tier two" words and are appropriate for instruction (Beck, McKeown, and Kucan 2002).

Root study promotes independent word learning (Carlisle 2010). In addition, roots are multipliers—that is, knowledge of one root can help determine the meaning, pronunciation, and spelling of 10, 20, or more English words. With roots, students learn to make connections among words that are semantically related (Nagy and Scott 2000). Research suggests that the brain is a pattern detector (Cunningham 2004). Roots follow linguistic patterns that help students with the meaning, sound, and spelling of English words. Indeed, Latin and Greek roots have consistent orthographic (spelling) patterns (Rasinski and Padak 2013; Bear et al. 2011).

Many English language learners speak first languages semantically related to Latin. For example, more than 75 percent of the words in Spanish come from Latin (Chandler and Schwartz 1961, 1991). Spanish, Portuguese, French, Catalan, Italian, and Rumanian are all classified as "Romance Languages" because they derive from Latin, the language of ancient Romans. Enhancing this natural linguistic connection inherent in many of these languages can accelerate these students' vocabulary growth (Blachowicz et al. 2006).

Many states are beginning to include a study of roots, including Latin and Greek derivations, in their elementary and middle school literacy standards. Indeed, the Common Core State Standards focus extensively on root-specific standards in the "Reading Foundational Skills" and "Language/Vocabulary Acquisition and Use" sections. According to these standards, attention to roots should begin in kindergarten.

prefix

A root at the beginning of a word. For example, in the word *circumference*, the initial *circum-* is a prefix, meaning "around."

base

The core root, which provides a word with its basic meaning. In the word *circumference*, the base is *fer-*, which means "bear," "go."

suffix

A root that ends a word. In the word *circumference*, the final *-ence* is a suffix, meaning "quality," "state," or "thing."

Note: You can find out more about what prefixes and suffixes do on the Digital Resource CD (filename: functions.pdf).

What Is a Root?

A *root* is a word part that contains meaning (and not merely sound). Roots are vocabulary multipliers—each root taught helps students discover the meaning to multiple words. The three types of roots, depending on their placement within a word, are a prefix, base, and suffix.

Mathematics Vocabulary Research and Practice *(cont.)*

Differentiating Instruction

Some students may need additional support. Others may benefit from additional challenge. These ideas may help you differentiate instruction:

- Use visual aids.

- Ask students to sketch or act out words. Others can guess the depicted words.

- Reduce length of activity.

- Pair students. Encourage them to talk about the roots and the activities.

- Challenge students to create new words that contain the root.

- Talk students through the necessary process to complete an activity. Your aim should be to scaffold students' thinking, not to provide answers.

- Alert other teachers (social studies, etc.) of the roots you are working on with students. Ask them to include them when possible in their own instruction with students.

- Have students keep a personal vocabulary journal in which they list the roots and related words they learn. Encourage students to use their new vocabulary in their oral and written language (e.g., "Use at least one word containing the [hyper-] root in your math journal entry today.")

- Put the roots and words derived from the roots on display in the classroom. (You may wish to move some of the displays into the hallway or other sites outside of your classroom.)

- Play word games that involve the roots with your students often. Word lists containing the roots in this book are found on the Digital Resource CD (filename: wordlists.pdf).

Students who need additional challenge can a) look for words containing the featured root in their content-area texts, b) write riddles for others to solve using several words that contain the root, or c) use an online resource to find additional words containing the root (e.g., http://www.onelook.com) or to create word puzzles featuring the root (e.g., http://www.puzzlemaker.com).

Like their peers, English language learners benefit from the focus on meaning using research-based strategies to learn new roots and words. Especially if students' native languages derive from Latin (e.g., Spanish), make comparisons to the native languages whenever possible. (You can look online for resources to assist with this.) When Spanish speakers learn to look for roots within words, they will be able to relate many word roots in English to their counterparts in Spanish. Sharing their knowledge with other classmates will help everyone grow.

How to Use This Book

The following information will help you implement each lesson.

Lesson Overview

A list of **Standards** (McREL and Common Core State Standards) is included in each lesson.

The **Materials** listed include the activity pages for students.

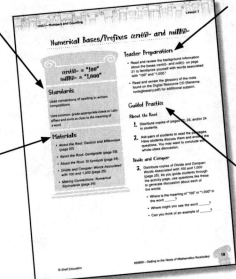

Each lesson begins with a **Teacher Preparation** that provides essential information about the root. Reading this section before you teach the lesson will provide you with a foundation to ensure student success.

The **Guided Practice** portion of each lesson includes suggestions for implementing each of the student activity pages.

Before beginning each lesson, review the **Teacher Background Information and Tips** page to provide additional help for students. Additional information to introduce each unit can be found on pages 12–13.

The **About the Root** activities are introductions and include short passages using the root of focus. The purpose of these passages is to show students contextual use of the root in mathematics. As students read to themselves or listen to the teacher read aloud, they identify words containing the roots in extended texts that center on a wide range of interesting topics.

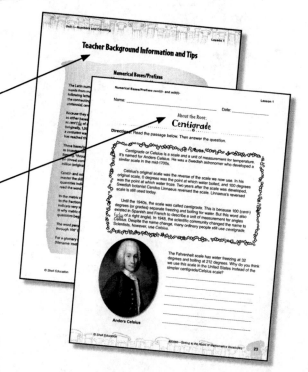

How to Use This Book *(cont.)*

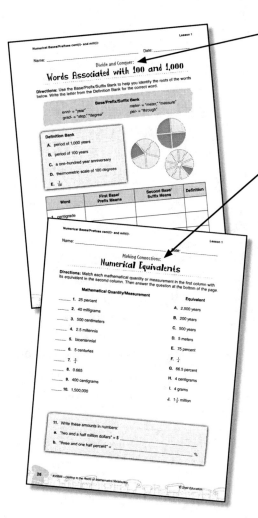

The **Divide and Conquer** activities allow students to pull words apart. They dissect the parts of the words, understand the meaning of these parts, and then gain a greater understanding of the word as a whole.

The **Making Connections** activities allow students to use their knowledge of roots to make connections to vocabulary and offer students the opportunity to extend their exploration of the root(s) through activities such as word sorts, riddles, representing the roots and related words in drawings, and game-like tasks. They may need to distinguish when to use a certain root, or which way the root is used in a word.

All of the student activity pages and additional resources such as word lists and flashcards can be found on the **Digital Resource CD**.

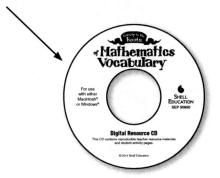

How to Use This Book (cont.)

Tips for Implementation

These tips will help you think about how to teach the lessons in this book.

- You will find many suggestions in this text, but remember that they are just that— suggestions. You should feel free to adapt the lessons to meet your students' needs.

- Plan to spend five to ten minutes per day on vocabulary related to mathematics.

- You can teach the lessons in any order. You may want to coordinate with your curriculum. Each lesson addresses one basic mathematical idea or concept. You can also expand on any lesson as you see fit. If students need more work on a particular root, you may wish to use some of the additional practice activities described in Appendix C.

- Before beginning a new lesson, read the Teacher Background Information and Tips page. These notes provide general information and identify many math words built on the base of the lesson.

- Talking about roots is very important for student learning. This approach to vocabulary development goes far beyond mere memorization of specific words (which, according to research, does not work). Students need to learn to think about how roots contribute to meanings. Talking this through can help them develop this realization. So, encourage students to talk, Talk, TALK!!!

- Each week, display the root(s) and meaning(s) prominently in your classroom. Encourage students to use the root as much as possible throughout the entire week. Reading, writing, speaking, and listening to words containing the root will facilitate learning. Several generic activities (see Appendix C) provide additional instruction or practice, if you or your students wish.

- You may wish to provide students with dictionaries as they work through the activities sheets.

How to Use This Book *(cont.)*

Introducing Each Unit

Refer to the following information before beginning each unit:

Unit I: Numbers and Counting

This unit presents eight roots that are essential to understanding the most basic mathematical concepts. The Teacher Background Information and Tips pages explain these math terms with reference to the abundant cognates generated by their roots.

Integers and *fractions* are built on the Latin bases meaning, respectively, "whole" and "broken." Just as a *fragment* is a broken piece, a *fraction* is a "broken" number. A person of *integrity* is of "whole" character, just as an *integer* is a "whole" number. The math terms of *finite* and *infinite* numbers, built on the Latin base meaning "end," "limit," "term," are cognates with such familiar words as *confine*, *definite*, and *final*. The mathematical operation of *converting* fractions and decimals are built on the Latin base *vers-*, *vert-*, meaning "turn," "change." Cognates from this base include such words as *reverse* and *advertise*. The geometric concept of a *transversal* is more easily understood when associated with the many *vers-*, *vert-* cognates that students may already know.

The Greek prefix *poly-* and its Latin equivalent *multi-*, meaning "many," are found in the mathematical vocabulary of *polygons* and *multiplication*. Students may already know these prefixes from everyday words such as *multimedia*, *multivitamin*, and *multitask*.

The Latin numerical bases, *cent(i)-* = "100" and *mill(i)-* = "1,000," generate everyday words such as *cents*, *century*, *century*, *million*, and *mile*. They are also important to understanding such terms as *milligram*, *centiliter*, and *milliliter*, words describing measurement in terms of $\frac{1}{100}$ and $\frac{1}{1,000}$. Because these two numerical bases are often found at the beginning of words, they may also be considered prefixes; we refer to them as "bases/prefixes."

Unit II: The "Basics" of Geometry

The terminology of geometry is largely based on both Greek and Latin roots. This unit presents seven bases that generate terms from geometry as well as many words from everyday and general academic vocabulary.

This unit contains vocabulary dealing with angles, polygons, and circles as well as with their classifications. Because "a picture is worth a thousand words," these lessons include a rich array of diagrams and line drawings to help students visualize the words they are encountering.

How to Use This Book (cont.)

Math in general can be challenging, but the roots approach helps students establish connections between this specific terminology and other words they may already know. By "rooting" the technical terminology of math and geometry in bases that generate other familiar vocabulary, students may more rapidly and comfortably understand and learn math concepts.

Unit III: "Parallel" Prefixes Indicating Spacial Relationships

One of the most important functions of a prefix is to indicate *direction*. This is why learning these prefixes can help students understand spatial relationships and the terminology we associate with geometrical figures:

* Greek *peri-* and Latin *circum-* = "around," as in *perimeter, circumference,* and *circumscribe*

* Greek *dia-* and Latin *per-* = "through," "across," "thorough," as in *diameter, diagonal, perpendicular,* and *percentage*

* Greek *syn-, sym-, syl-* and Latin *co-, con-, com-* = "with," "together," "very," as in *symmetrical, synchronize, coordinates, converge, concentric,* and *compound*

* Greek *hypo-* and Latin *sub-* = "under," "below," as in *hypothesis, hypotenuse, hypocenter, subtract, subdivide, subtotal,* and *subset*

* Greek *hyper-* and Latin *super-, sur-* = "over," "above," as in *hypertension, hyperthermia, superimpose, supernumerary,* and *surcharge*

Unit IV: Measuring and Metrics

This unit presents vocabulary dealing with measurement and the metric system. We begin with words containing the Greek base *meter-, metr-,* which means "measure" in words from general vocabulary. Students practice dividing and conquering such technical words as *odometer, barometer, pedometer, metronome, perimeter, symmetry,* and *diameter.*

The subsequent lessons present the vocabulary of the *metric system.* Since the metric system is based on units of 10, 100, and 1,000, we present the Greek and Latin numerical bases/prefixes for these numbers.

Numerical bases *dec(i)-, cent(i)-,* and *mill(i)-* are used in words that indicate fractions of meters, grams, and liters. Metric-system terminology employing Latin numerical bases, therefore, indicate small units of measurement.

Greek numerical bases, by contrast, are used in words that indicate multiples of meters, grams, and liters. Metric-system words employing Greek numerical bases, therefore, indicate large units of measurement.

How to Use This Book (cont.)

Introducing Each Lesson

Introduce each root by linking to words students already know. You could:

* Put two or three common words containing the root on the board and ask students to talk about what meaning they share. You may want to embed these words in phrases or include quick sketches, if applicable. By perusing the Teacher Background Information and Tips section in each lesson, you will readily find a large number of derivatives. Select words that you think your students will recognize.

* Tell students, "The root of the week is _____ . It means _____." Ask them to work with partners to generate words containing the root. Make a class list, and discuss common meaning.

* Encourage students to use the root's definition in their talk about words containing the root.

Assessment

At least one part of each lesson could be used for assessment purposes. Suggestions for assessment include:

* Use a knowledge rating chart with students. To do this, select key words from something students will read. Make a three-column chart for students to indicate if they a) know a word well, b) have seen or heard it, or c) don't know it at all.

* Have students keep word journals in which they a) record information about roots and the words that contain them or b) keep lists of interesting words from their reading. Ask students to peruse their journals occasionally to draw some conclusions about their word knowledge.

* Encourage students to use self-assessment. Ask them to write about a) their own word knowledge, b) where they find new and interesting words, and/or c) what strategies they use most often to figure out the meaning of new words.

Correlation to the Standards

Shell Education is committed to producing educational materials that are research and standards based. In this effort, we have correlated all of our products to the academic standards of all 50 United States, the District of Columbia, the Department of Defense Dependent Schools, and all Canadian provinces.

How To Find Standards Correlations

To print a customized correlation report of this product for your state, visit our website at http://www.shelleducation.com and follow the on-screen directions. If you require assistance in printing correlation reports, please contact Customer Service at 1-877-777-3450.

Purpose and Intent of Standards

Legislation mandates that all states adopt academic standards that identify the skills students will learn in kindergarten through grade twelve. Many states also have standards for Pre–K. This same legislation sets requirements to ensure the standards are detailed and comprehensive.

Standards are designed to focus instruction and guide adoption of curricula. Standards are statements that describe the criteria necessary for students to meet specific academic goals. They define the knowledge, skills, and content students should acquire at each level. Standards are also used to develop standardized tests to evaluate students' academic progress. Teachers are required to demonstrate how their lessons meet state standards. State standards are used in the development of all of our products, so educators can be assured they meet the academic requirements of each state.

Common Core State Standards

Many lessons in this book are aligned to the Common Core State Standards (CCSS). The standards support the objectives presented throughout the lessons and are provided on the Digital Resource CD (filename: standards.pdf).

McREL Compendium

We use the Mid-continent Research for Education and Learning (McREL) Compendium to create standards correlations. Each year, McREL analyzes state standards and revises the compendium. By following this procedure, McREL is able to produce a general compilation of national standards. Each lesson in this product is based on one or more McREL standards, which are provided on the Digital Resource CD (filename: standards.pdf).

TESOL and WIDA Standards

The lessons in this book promote English language development for English language learners. The standards listed on the Digital Resource CD (filename: standards.pdf) support the language objectives presented throughout the lessons.

Standards Chart

Common Core State Standard	Page(s)
Literacy L.6-8.4b—Use common, grade-appropriate Greek or Latin affixes and roots as clues to the meaning of a word	All Lessons
Literacy RI.6-8.4—Determine the meaning of words and phrases as they are used in a text, including figurative, connotative, and technical meanings	All Lessons
Literacy RI.6-8.10—By the end of the year, read and comprehend literary nonfiction in the grades 6–8 text complexity band proficiently, with scaffolding as needed at the high end of the range	All Lessons

Concept Correlations

The following lessons are especially useful during the instruction of the concepts listed below.

Concept	Lessons
Numbers (Prime and Composite)	Unit I: Lesson 1
Fractions (Proper and Improper)	Unit I: Lesson 3 and Lesson 5
Numbers (Finite and Infinite)	Unit I: Lesson 4
Conversion of Fractions and Decimals	Unit I: Lesson 5
Angles	Unit II: Lesson 1 and Lesson 2
Polygons	Unit I: Lesson 2; Unit II: Lesson 1 and Lesson 2
Geometric Figures	Unit I: Lesson 2 and Lesson 5; Unit II: Lesson 1, Lesson 2, Lesson 3, and Lesson 5; Unit III: Lesson 1, Lesson 2, and Lesson 4
Measurement	Unit III: Lesson 1 and Lesson 5; Unit IV: Lesson 1, Lesson 2, Lesson 3, Lesson 4 and Lesson 5
Symmetry	Unit III: Lesson 3

About the Authors

Timothy Rasinski, Ph.D., is a professor of literacy education at Kent State University. He has written over 150 articles and has authored, coauthored, or edited over 15 books and curriculum programs on reading education. His research on reading has been cited by the National Reading Panel and has been published in journals such as *Reading Research Quarterly*, *The Reading Teacher*, *Reading Psychology*, and *The Journal of Educational Research*. Tim served on the Board of Directors of the International Reading Association, and from 1992–1999, he was coeditor of *The Reading Teacher*, the world's most widely read journal of literacy education. He has also served as editor of the *Journal of Literacy Research*, one of the premier research journals in reading. Tim is a past president of the College Reading Association, and he has won the A.B. Herr Award from the College Reading Association for his scholarly contributions to literacy education. In 2010, Tim was elected into the International Reading Hall of Fame.

Nancy Padak, Ed.D., is an active researcher, author, and consultant. She was a Distinguished Professor in the College and Graduate School of Education, Health, and Human Services at Kent State University. She directed KSU's Reading and Writing Center and taught in the area of literacy education. She was the Principal Investigator for the Ohio Literacy Resource Center, which has provided support for adult and family literacy programs since 1993. Prior to her arrival at Kent State in 1985, she was a classroom teacher and district administrator. She has written or edited more than 25 books and more than 90 chapters and articles. She has also served in a variety of leadership roles in professional organizations, including the presidency of the College Reading Association and (with others) the Editor of *The Reading Teacher* and the *Journal of Literacy Research*. She has won several awards for her scholarship and contributions to literacy education.

About the Authors *(cont.)*

Rick M. Newton, Ph.D., holds a doctoral degree in Greek and Latin from the University of Michigan and is now an emeritus professor of Greek and Latin at Kent State University. He developed the course "English Words from Classical Elements," which more than 15,000 Kent State students have taken over the past 30 years. He holds the Distinguished Teaching Award from the Kent State College of Arts and Sciences and the Translation Award from the Modern Greek Studies Association of North America and Canada.

Evangeline Newton, Ph.D., is a professor of literacy education at the University of Akron, where she served as the first director of the Center for Literacy. She teaches a variety of literacy methods courses and professional development workshops to elementary, middle, and high school teachers. A former coeditor of *The Ohio Reading Teacher*, Evangeline currently chairs the Reading Review Board of the Ohio Resource Center for Mathematics, Science, and Reading. She serves on editorial review boards for *The Reading Teacher* and *Reading Horizons*. Evangeline is active in the Association of Literacy Educators and the International Reading Association (IRA). As a participant in IRA's Reading and Writing for Critical Thinking project, Evangeline taught workshops for teachers and Peace Corps volunteers in Armenia. A former St. Louis public school teacher, Evangeline holds a B.A. from Washington University in St. Louis, an M.A.T. from Webster University, and a Ph.D. from Kent State University.

Numerical Bases/Prefixes *cent(i)-* and *mill(i)-*

cent(i)- = "100"
mill(i)- = "1,000"

Standards

Uses conventions of spelling in written compositions

Uses common, grade-appropriate Greek or Latin affixes and roots as clues to the meaning of a word

Materials

- *About the Root: Century and Millennium* (page 22)

- *About the Root: Centigrade* (page 23)

- *About the Root: SI Symbols* (page 24)

- *Divide and Conquer: Words Associated with 100 and 1,000* (page 25)

- *Making Connections: Numerical Equivalents* (page 26)

Teacher Preparation

- Read and review the background information about the bases *cent(i)-* and *mill(i)-* on page 21 to familiarize yourself with words associated with "100" and "1,000."

- Read and review the glossary of the roots found on the Digital Resource CD (filename: rootsglossary.pdf) for additional support.

Guided Practice

About the Root

1. Distribute copies of pages 22, 23, and/or 24 to students.

2. Ask pairs of students to read the passages. Have students discuss them and answer the questions. You may want to conclude with whole-class discussion.

Divide and Conquer

3. Distribute copies of *Divide and Conquer: Words Associated with 100 and 1,000* (page 25). As you guide students through the activity page, use questions like these to generate discussion about each of the words:

   - Where is the meaning of "100" or "1,000" in the word _____?

   - Where might you see the word _____?

   - Can you think of an example of _____?

Numerical Bases/Prefixes cent(i)- and mill(i)- (cont.)

Making Connections

4. Distribute copies of *Making Connections: Numerical Equivalents* (page 26).

5. Ask students to skim the page before completing the activity sheet.

6. To conclude this activity, ask students, "Which items were most challenging?" Then, follow up mathematically on these items.

Words with cent(i)- and mill(i)-

bicentennial

billion

billionaire

centenarian

centennial

centigrade

centigram

centipede

centurion

century

percent

sesquicentennial

tricentennial

mile

millennium

milliliter

millimeter

million

millionaire

millipede

mills

multimillionaire

trillion

trillionaire

A list of words to print out for students can be found on the Digital Resource CD (filename: wordlists.pdf).

Did you know...

Billion is a contracted form of *bimillion* (i.e., 1,000,000,000). *Trillion* is contracted from *trimillion*. The word *million* means 1,000 units of 1,000. Hence, a billion is two units, a trillion is three units, a quadrillion is four, etc. All of these words are formed by analogy with million. The nonsense word *zillion*, citing the last letter of the alphabet, refers to the highest possible number.

Teacher Background Information and Tips

Numerical Bases/Prefixes
cent(i)- = "100" and mill(i)- = "1,000"

The Latin numerical roots *cent(i)-* = "100" and *mill(i)-* = "1,000" appear in a large number of words from math. The connecting *i* at the end of these Latin bases/prefixes is used if the following letter in the word is a consonant (e.g., *centigram, centipede, millimeter, milliliter*); the connecting *i* is not necessary if the following letter in the word is a vowel (e.g., *centennial, century, millennium, millionaire*).

Because they often appear at the beginning of words, *cent(i)-* and *mill(i)-* may be classified as either bases or prefixes. These bases/prefixes provide the base meaning of such words as *cent* ($\frac{1}{100}$ of a dollar), *century* (a span of 100 years), *million* (1,000 x 1,000), and *mile* (originally, 1,000 paces as marched by a wide-stepping Roman soldier). In the Roman army, a *centurion* was an officer placed in charge of 100 soldiers. A *centenarian* is a person who has reached the age of 100.

These bases/prefixes may also be preceded by other prefixes. *Cent(i)-* occurs in such words as *bicentennial* (a 200-year anniversary), *percent* (a whole divided into 100 equal parts; literally, "through 100," *per* cent[um]), and *sesquicentennial*. The Latin prefixes *bi-* (two) and *tri-* (three) combine with *mill(i)-* to produce the words *billion* (originally "bi-million") and *trillion* (originally "tri-million").

Cent(i)- and *mill(i)-* generate a large number of words through which students can readily master the skill of "dividing and conquering" vocabulary. As they identify the numerical quantities indicated by the prefixes and bases, they simply count the quantities as they read the word.

In the metric system, *cent(i)-* and *mill(i)-* refer not to multiples of 100 and 1,000 but, rather, to the fractions $\frac{1}{100}$ and $\frac{1}{1,000}$. Metric-system words beginning with these bases/prefixes indicate very small quantities and lengths: *cent(i)-* means $\frac{1}{100}$, and *mill(i)-* means $\frac{1}{1,000}$. This is why metric quantities beginning with *mill(i)-* are smaller (actually, ten times smaller) than quantities beginning with *cent(i)-*. (See Unit IV for more on this.)

The word *percent* (originally written as a two-word phrase, *per cent*) means "distributed through 100" (Latin prefix *per-* = "through"; thus, the symbol % = $\frac{1}{100}$).

For a glossary of words built on these roots, see the Digital Resource CD (filename: rootsglossary.pdf).

Name: _____   Date: _____

About the Root:
Century and Millennium

Directions: Read the information below. Then answer the questions.

> This lesson focuses on two Latin numerical roots. *Cent(i)-* means "100," and *mill(i)-* means "1,000." Words built on these roots appear in a large number of math words. The connecting *i* at the end of these Latin bases/prefixes is used if the following letter in the word is a consonant (e.g., *centigram, millimeter*). The connecting *i* is not necessary if the following letter in the word is a vowel (e.g., *centennial, millennium*).

1. How many years are there in a *century*? How do you know?

   _____

   _____

2. How many years are there in a *millennium*? How do you know?

   _____

   _____

Name: _____   Date: _____

About the Root:
Centigrade
....

Directions: Read the passage below. Then answer the question.

Centigrade or Celsius is a scale and a unit of measurement for temperature. It's named for Anders Celsius. He was a Swedish astronomer who developed a similar scale in the mid-1700s.

Celsius's original scale was the reverse of the scale we now use. In his original scale, 0 degrees was the point at which water boiled, and 100 degrees was the point at which water froze. Two years after the scale was developed, Swedish botanist Carolus Linnaeus reversed the scale. Linnaeus's reversed scale is still used today.

Until the 1940s, the scale was called *centigrade*. This is because 100 (*cent-*) degrees (or grades) separate freezing and boiling for water. But this word also existed in Spanish and French to describe a unit of measurement for angles ($\frac{1}{10,000}$ of a right angle). In 1948, the scientific community changed the name to *Celsius*. Despite the name change, many ordinary people still use *centigrade*. Scientists, however, use *Celsius*.

Anders Celsius

The Fahrenheit scale has water freezing at 32 degrees and boiling at 212 degrees. Why do you think we use this scale in the United States instead of the simpler centigrade/Celsius scale?

_____

_____

_____

_____

_____

_____

Name: _____   Date: _____

About the Root:
SI Symbols

. . . .

Directions: Read the passage below. Then answer the questions.

The International System of Units has developed a set of prefixes called *SI prefixes,* or metric prefixes. Like all prefixes, they come before a basic unit of measure. The prefixes refer to multiples of the measure or fractions of the measure. The International Bureau of Weights and Measures standardized these prefixes. Some prefixes date back to the development of the metric system in the 1790s.

Using the prefixes allows us to refer to very large or very small measures without using all the zeroes. For example, suppose you needed to refer to a very tiny grain of sand, a grain so small that it weighed only a billionth of a gram. You could write 0.000 000 001 gram. Or you could use the SI prefix *nano*, which means "a billionth," and write a *nanogram*.

The prefixes near zero are the oldest. These date from the development of the metric system (1795):

◎ kilo (k) = 1,000   ◎ deci (d) = tenth

◎ hecto (h) = 100   ◎ centi (c) = hundredth

◎ deca (da) = 10   ◎ milli (m) = thousandth

The largest and smallest prefixes are the newest. The prefix *yotta* (Y), for example, refers to a septillion—1 followed by 24 zeroes! And the prefix *yocto* (y) refers to a septillionth, a decimal with the 1 24 places away from the decimal point. These were established in 1991.

Why do you think prefixes for very large or very small measures are newer than other prefixes? For example, why is *yocto-* (from 1991) newer than *centi-* or *milli-* (from 1795)?

_____

_____

_____

Name: _____ Date: _____

Divide and Conquer:
Words Associated with 100 and 1,000

Directions: Use the Base/Prefix/Suffix Bank to help you identify the roots of the words below. Write the letter from the Definition Bank for the correct word.

Base/Prefix/Suffix Bank

enni- = "year"   *meter-* = "meter," "measure"
grad- = "step," "degree"   *per-* = "through"

Definition Bank

A. period of 1,000 years

B. period of 100 years

C. a one-hundred year anniversary

D. thermometric scale of 100 degrees

E. $\frac{1}{100}$

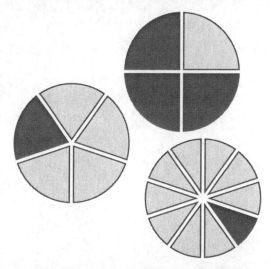

Word	First Base/ Prefix Means	Second Base/ Suffix Means	Definition
1. centigrade			
2. percent			
3. century			
4. centennial			
5. millennium			

Name: _____   Date: _____

Making Connections:
Numerical Equivalents

Directions: Match each mathematical quantity or measurement in the first column with its equivalent in the second column. Then answer the question at the bottom of the page.

Mathematical Quantity/Measurement

_____ **1.** 25 percent

_____ **2.** 40 milligrams

_____ **3.** 500 centimeters

_____ **4.** 2.5 millennia

_____ **5.** bicentennial

_____ **6.** 5 centuries

_____ **7.** $\frac{3}{4}$

_____ **8.** 0.665

_____ **9.** 400 centigrams

_____ **10.** 1,500,000

Equivalent

A. 2,500 years

B. 200 years

C. 500 years

D. 5 meters

E. 75 percent

F. $\frac{1}{4}$

G. 66.5 percent

H. 4 centigrams

I. 4 grams

J. $1\frac{1}{2}$ million

11. Write these amounts in numbers:

a. "two and a half million dollars" = $ _____

b. "three and one half percent" = _____ %

Prefixes *poly-* and *multi-*

poly-, multi- = "many"

Standards

Uses a variety of strategies to extend reading vocabulary

Determines the meaning of words and phrases as they are used in a text, including figurative, connotative, and technical meanings

Materials

- *About the Root: Many Words* (page 30)
- *About the Root: Multiplication* (page 31)
- *About the Root: Polygons* (page 32)
- *Divide and Conquer: Words Associated with Many* (page 33)
- *Making Connections: Who/What Are We?* (page 34)

Teacher Preparation

- Read and review the background information about the prefixes *poly-* and *multi-* on page 29 to familiarize yourself with words associated with "many."

- Read and review the glossary of the roots found on the Digital Resource CD (filename: rootsglossary.pdf) for additional support.

Guided Practice

About the Root

1. Distribute copies of pages 30, 31, and/or 32 to students.

2. Write *poly-* and *multi-* on the board. Tell students that these prefixes mean "many." Ask partners to think about words they already know with these prefixes. Invite whole-group discussion.

3. With partners, ask students to read the passages and answer the questions.

4. Conclude with another whole-class discussion.

Divide and Conquer

5. Distribute copies of *Divide and Conquer: Words Associated with Many* (page 33). As you guide students through the activity page, use questions like these to generate discussion about each of the words:

- Where is the meaning of "many" in the word _____?
- Where might you see the word _____?
- Can you think of an example of _____?

Prefixes *poly-* and *multi-* (cont.)

Making Connections

6. Distribute copies of *Making Connections: Who/What Are We?* (page 34). Ask students to read all of the definitions before completing the activity sheet.

7. You might conclude with a discussion that focuses on root meaning.

Words with *poly-* and *multi-*

polygamist

polygamy

polygon

polygonal

polypod

polytheism

polytheist

multicolored

multicultural

multiculturalism

multilateral

multilingual

multimedia

multimillionaire

multipartite

multiple

multiply

multiplication

multitask

multitude

multivitamin

A list of words to print out for students can be found on the Digital Resource CD (filename: wordlists.pdf).

Teacher Background Information and Tips

Prefixes *poly-* and *multi-* = "many"

The Greek prefix *poly-* and the Latin prefix *multi-* mean "many" and appear in words that express two basic mathematical concepts and operations. *Poly-* appears in the word *polygon*. *Multi-* appears in the words *multiple*, *multiply*, and *multiplication*.

Built on the Latin base *ply-*, *plic-*, meaning "fold" (e.g., *ply*wood consists of multiple folds of panels), the words *multiply* and *multiplication* describe the "manifold" process of adding numbers. This is why we sometimes call *multiplication* "shorthand addition." When we multiply, we *apply* the same number many times over. Thus, instead of writing the number 2 five times (2 + 2 + 2 + 2 + 2 = 10), we simply multiply 2 x 5 = 10. The number resulting from *multiplication* is called the *product*.

Prefixes *multi-* and *poly-* generate many non-math words that students may already know (e.g., *multivitamin*, *multilateral*, *polytheist*). Reviewing some of these words may help students better retain the meaning of "many" in them.

Although most students identify a *polygon* as a figure with many sides, this word actually means "a figure with many angles" (Greek base *gon-* = "angle," "corner"). Because a *polygon* has as many sides as it has angles, the definitions are essentially the same. Observe the interesting distinction that we call four-sided polygons *quadrilaterals* (four-sided figures), using Latin roots (and not "tetragons," which would be the Greek-based equivalent; but we do use the adjectival form *tetragonal* to describe aspects of *quadrilaterals*). We also call them *quadrangles* (four-angled figures). In geometry, *polygons* are named according to the number of their sides or angles (e.g., *triangle*, *pentagon*).

Polygons are classified according to the degrees of their angles. In a *convex polygon*, every internal angle is equal to or less than 180 degrees. Because the "points" of a regular *polygon's* corners (called *vertices*, the plural of *vertex:* see Lesson 5 of this Unit) all point away from the center, a *regular polygon* has a *convex* shape.

In a *concave polygon*, one or more angles must be a reflex angle (i.e., greater than 180 degrees). Built on the Latin base *flex-* ("bend") and the Latin prefix *re-* ("back," "again"), a *reflex angle* appears as if it is "bent back" and opens out.

The understanding that a *polygon* has the same number of sides as it has angles is a basic concept. Equal angles within a *polygon* have corresponding sides of equal length. Thus, an *equilateral triangle* is also an *equiangular triangle*. In geometry, we refer to equal angles as *congruent angles*. Equal line segments are called *congruent line segments*. The adjective *congruent* is of Latin origin, meaning "coming together," "agreeing."

For a glossary of words built on these roots, see the Digital Resource CD (filename: rootsglossary.pdf).

Name: _____   Date: _____

About the Root:
Many Words

. . . .

Directions: Read the information below. Then answer the questions.

> The Greek prefix *poly-* and the Latin prefix *multi-* mean "many." These prefixes appear in math words and also general vocabulary words. If you have ever seen a stop sign, for example, you may have noticed that it is shaped like a *polygon*. When people try to do many things at the same time, we say that they *multitask*. People who speak more than one language are called *multilingual*.

◎ How does the word *multivitamin* express the idea of "many"?

_____

_____

◎ Why might a centipede be called a *polypod*?

_____

_____

◎ Why do you think *multiplex* movie theaters are so popular?

_____

_____

◎ Do you like wearing *multicolored* clothes?

_____

_____

◎ Can you give an example of a *polysyllabic* word?

_____

Name: _____ Date: _____

About the Root:
Multiplication

Directions: Read the passage below. Then solve the problem.

You know how to *multiply*, but did you ever think about the ideas behind *multiplication*? Multiplication is the process of scaling one number by another (adding a number to itself several times). Here's a way to think about this scaling. Imagine 12 marbles—3 red, 3 blue, 3 yellow, and 3 green—in 4 bags. We could scale the number of bags by the number of marbles per bag (3 + 3 + 3 + 3 = 12 or 4 [bags] x 3 [marbles per bag] = 12 [marbles]). Seen this way, multiplication is a more efficient means of addition.

Several ancient civilizations used multiplication. Ancient Babylonians used a positional number system somewhat like our modern decimal system. They also developed multiplication tables to use as "cheat sheets." Ancient Chinese mathematicians wrote multiplication problems out in words. They also used "rod calculus," counting rods that predated the abacus. With these rods, they were able to add, subtract, multiply, and divide and also to deal with place value.

Mathematicians have established several properties that apply to multiplication. For example, any number multiplied by zero is zero. Likewise, any number multiplied by 1 is the number itself. Finally, the order of terms in a multiplication problem doesn't matter. A x B is the same as B x A.

Make up a word problem that deals with two groups of four. Then solve the problem using a) addition and b) multiplication.

Word Problem: _____

_____

_____

Addition: _____ Multiplication: _____

Name: _____ Date: _____

About the Root:
Polygons

Directions: Read the passage below. Then answer the questions.

Have you ever looked closely at a honeycomb? If so, you have seen a *polygon* in nature. The small bits of wax in honeycombs are shaped like hexagons. A hexagon is one type of polygon.

A polygon is a flat (two-dimensional) shape made of straight lines that are joined. The lines in a polygon are called *segments*. These segments enclose a space. In simple polygons, the segments do not intersect. (Complex polygons have intersecting lines.) The number of sides is the name of the particular simple polygon—triangle, quadrilateral, octagon, and so forth.

Several other natural examples of polygons exist. Crystals have flat faces or facets that are polygons. Sea stars, found in oceans, are pentagons. The next time you're in the grocery store, look for star fruit. A cross section of a star fruit is also a pentagon.

◎ Draw 2 simple polygons. Then write about how you know they are polygons on a separate sheet of paper.

◎ Draw a polygon with segments that intersect. How many simple polygons are part of this larger polygon? Number the simple polygons.

Name: _____ Date: _____

Divide and Conquer:
Words Associated with Many

Directions: Use the Base/Prefix/Suffix Bank to help you identify the roots of the words below. Write the letter from the Definition Bank for the correct word.

Base/Prefix/Suffix Bank

gon- = "angle," "corner"	*part-* = "part"	*the-* = "god"
later- = "side"	*ply-, pli-* = "fold"	

Definition Bank

A. consisting of many parts

B. consisting of many sides

C. one who believes in multiple gods or deities

D. a geometric figure with many sides and angles

E. the number by which another number is multiplied

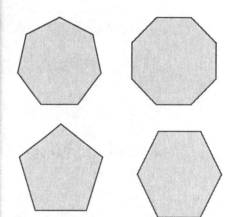

Word	First Base/ Prefix Means	Second Base/ Suffix Means	Definition
1. multilateral			
2. polygon			
3. multiplier			
4. polytheist			
5. multipartite			

Name: _____   Date: _____

Making Connections:
Who/What Are We?

· ·

Directions: Match each math and general-vocabulary word or phrase in the first column with the sample listed in the second column.

Concept	**Sample**
_____ 1. trilateral polygons	**A.** rectangle, parallelogram, pentagon, hexagon
_____ 2. regular rectangle	**B.** equilateral triangle
_____ 3. equilateral quadrangles	**C.** isosceles triangle, equilateral triangle, right triangle, scalene triangle
_____ 4. regular triangle	**D.** square and rhombus
_____ 5. polygonal figures	**E.** square
_____ 6. computing the perimeter of a polygon	**F.** add the lengths of all sides
_____ 7. multilateral	**G.** having many sides
_____ 8. polygon	**H.** any 2-dimensional shape that consists of straight lines that are joined

9. Below is an isosceles triangle. Mark the two equal sides. Is this figure multilateral? Explain.

A

C   B

_____

_____

_____

Bases *integer-, integr-* and *frag-, fract-*

integer-, integr- = "whole"
frag-, fract- = "break," "broken"

Standards

Uses conventions of spelling in written compositions

By the end of the year, reads and comprehends literary nonfiction in the grades 6–8 text complexity band proficiently, with scaffolding as needed at the high end of the range

Materials

- *About the Root: Categorizing Numbers* (page 38)

- *About the Root: What Is an Integer?* (page 39)

- *About the Root: What Is a Fractal?* (page 40)

- *Divide and Conquer: Words Associated with Whole and Broken* (page 41)

- *Making Connections: Magic Square* (page 42)

Teacher Preparation

- Read and review the background information about the bases *integer-, integr-, frag-, fract-* on page 37 to familiarize yourself with words associated with "whole" and "broken."

- Read and review the glossary of the bases found on the Digital Resource CD (filename: rootsglossary.pdf) for additional support.

Guided Practice

About the Root

1. Distribute copies of pages 38, 39, and/or 40 to students.

2. Write *integer-, integr-* = "whole" and *frag-, fract-* = "break," "broken" on the board. Tell students that these bases are the focus of the next few lessons.

3. Ask students to read the passages and answer the questions alone or with a partner. You may want to conclude with whole-class discussion, including asking students to brainstorm other words containing these roots.

Bases *integer-, integr-* and *frag-, fract-* (cont.)

Divide and Conquer

4. Distribute copies of *Divide and Conquer: Words Associated with Whole and Broken* (page 41). As you guide students through the activity page, use questions like these to generate discussion about each of the words:

- Where is the meaning of "whole," "break," or "broken" in the word _____?

- Where might you see the word _____?

- Can you think of an example of _____?

Making Connections

5. Distribute copies of *Making Connections: Magic Square* (page 42).

6. Ask students to read all of the definitions before completing the activity.

7. Conclude with a discussion that focuses on root meaning. You could also help students understand any of the math that puzzled them.

Words with *integer-, integr-* and *frag-, fract-*

disintegrate
integers
integral
integrate
integration
integrity
diffract
fractals
fraction
fractious
fracture
fragile
fragment
fragmentary
fragmentation
infraction
infringe
infringement
refraction

A list of words to print out for students can be found on the Digital Resource CD (filename: wordlists.pdf).

Teacher Background Information and Tips

Bases *integer-, integr-* = "whole" and *frag-, fract-* = "break," "broken"

The Latin bases *integer-, integr-* = "whole" and *frag-, fract-* = "break," "broken" provide the foundation for one of the most basic of all mathematical concepts: the classification of numbers. We categorize "whole" numbers as *integers,* and we categorize "broken" numbers as *fractions.* The horizontal line separating the numerator from the denominator provides an excellent visual reminder that *fractions* are, by definition, "broken" numbers. *Integers* include positive whole numbers, zero, and negative whole numbers.

Students may already know words built on these two bases from everyday vocabulary or from general academic vocabulary. They may be familiar with such words as *fragile* (easily breakable), *fragment* (a piece broken off from an object), and *fracture* (the internal breaking or cracking of bones). They may also know the word *infraction,* which describes the violation or breaking of a rule or law. By associating the mathematical term *fraction* with these cognates, students may better comprehend the concept of "broken numbers."

Students may also know words built on the *integer-, integr-* base, although they may not associate these words with "wholeness." We say that a person of solid and whole character possesses *integrity.* An *integral* member of a group is essential to that group's wholeness. Likewise, in social studies, the principle of *integration* deals with the "wholeness" of a society not broken along racial, ethnic, or religious lines of division. When things fall apart from a whole state, we say that they *disintegrate* (Latin prefix *dis-* = "apart," "in different directions," "not"). Some of these nonmathematical terms may help students better understand that *integers* are "whole" numbers.

One of the more recent terms in mathematics is *fractals.* This term was coined in 1975 by French mathematician Benoit Mandelbrot, who went back to Latin roots for the name. Built on the Latin base for "break," a *fractal* is a piece broken off from the whole which displays identical, or nearly identical, patterns and shapes as the whole from which it is taken. *Fractals* occur in botany (such as patterns in leaves), geology (coastline fractals), zoology (the designs of a seashell), geometry (fractal geometry), physics (the symmetrical diffraction of images in a kaleidoscope), and statistics (economic patterns). *Fractal art* produces designs based on the *fractals* that occur in the natural world.

For a glossary of words built on these roots, see the Digital Resource CD (filename: rootsglossary.pdf).

Name: _____   Date: _____

About the Root:
Categorizing Numbers

Directions: Read the information below. Then answer the questions.

$\dfrac{2}{5}$

-3

$\dfrac{3}{4}$

The Latin base *integer-*, *integr-* means "whole." The Latin base *frag-*, *fract-* means "break," "broken." These two bases provide the foundation for a basic mathematical concept—the classification of numbers. We categorize "whole" numbers as *integers,* and we categorize "broken" numbers as *fractions.* You may already know the word *fracture*, which describes a "break" inside a bone.

$\dfrac{1}{5}$

7

$\dfrac{3}{7}$

◎ How does the word *integer* reflect the idea of "wholeness"?

_____

_____

◎ Can you figure out what a chef does when he or she *integrates* the dry and wet ingredients in a recipe?

_____

_____

◎ How does the word *fraction* reflect the idea of being "broken"?

_____

_____

◎ Can you figure out what a *fragment* of pottery is?

_____

_____

Name: _____   Date: _____

About the Root:
What Is an Integer?
. . . .

Directions: Read the passage below. Then answer the question.

A Mother Goose rhyme starts, "One, two, three, four, five. Once I caught a fish alive." The numbers in this rhyme are *integers*. Integers are natural numbers, including zero, that can be written without fractions or decimals. Integers can be positive or negative. They are equally spaced on a line. That is, the distance between 1 and 2 is the same as the distance between 87 and 88 or −43 and −42.

Mathematicians have described some properties that describe how integers work. If you add two integers—any two integers—together, the answer will always be an integer. The same is true of multiplication and subtraction. This does not work for division, however. If you divide 1 by 2, the answer is $\frac{1}{2}$ or 0.5. This is not an integer. Besides that, we cannot divide by zero, and zero is an integer.

Integers are helpful in arithmetic and algebra. They are also important in computer science. Computer languages are binary—based on 0 and 1—integers!

Make a math problem that shows how adding two integers results in another integer. Then do the same for multiplication and subtraction. Write a sentence explaining how you know your answers are integers.

addition	multiplication	subtraction

_____

_____

Name: _____　Date: _____

About the Root:
What Is a Fractal?

Directions: Read the passage below. Then answer the question.

Ferns grow in damp, shady areas. They are sometimes added to flower arrangements. The next time you see a fern, look carefully at the tiny leaves that make it up. Look also at the shape of the entire frond or fern leaf. You will see that the tiny leaves are exactly the same shape as the larger frond. This is a *fractal* found in nature.

Fractals are a new branch of math (and art). Search for pictures of fractals on a computer, and you will see their beauty. Fractal geometry can be used to describe things found in nature, such as coastlines, mountains, and even parts of living organisms. These things cannot easily be described using Euclidian geometry, which relies on regular shapes such as points, lines, and planes.

One property of fractals is self-similarity. The entire fractal, like the entire fern frond, is made up of tinier and tinier pieces of exactly the same shape.

Mathematicians believe that cartographers in Great Britain discovered the principles of fractals many years ago. They were trying to measure the coast of Great Britain. They noticed that the closer they looked, the more detailed and longer the coastline appeared to become.

The invention of computers and computer graphic programs has made it possible for all of us to see fractals. Computers can generate fractals, but geometric equations drive them. Fractal geometry offers almost unlimited ways to describe, measure, and predict natural phenomena.

Why do you think computers were so important in the development of fractal geometry?

_____

_____

_____

Name: _____   Date: _____

Divide and Conquer:
Words Associated with Whole and Broken

Directions: Use the Base/Prefix/Suffix Bank to help you identify the roots of the words below. *X* means the word does not contain that element. Write the letter from the Definition Bank for the correct word. The *-ional* suffix makes one of the words an adjective.

Base/Prefix/Suffix Bank

in- = "in," "on," "into"   *-ment* = "thing"   *ion-* = "thing"

Definition Bank

A. to incorporate into a larger unit

B. a partial number

C. very small; describing a fraction

D. a broken piece

E. a whole number

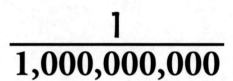

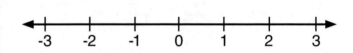

Word	First Base/Prefix Means	Second Base/Suffix Means	Definition
1. fragment			
2. integer		X	
3. fraction			
4. integrate		X	
5. fractional			

Name: _____   Date: _____

Making Connections:
Magic Square

Directions: Match items in the left column with items in the right column. Put the number of each answer in the corresponding box in the magic square. You can check your answers. The sum of each row and each column will be the same "magic" number. You will not use one number.

_____ **A.** negative numbers	**1.** 13, 17, 15, 21, 19
_____ **B.** proper fractions	**2.** –2, –7, –121
_____ **C.** simplified fractions	**3.** 2, 3, 5, 7, 11, 13
_____ **D.** improper fractions	**4.** 51, 52, 53
_____ **E.** mixed numbers	**5.** 4, 6, 8, 9, 10
_____ **F.** consecutive integers	**6.** $\frac{8}{3}$, $\frac{12}{10}$, $\frac{9}{6}$
_____ **G.** natural number	**7.** $\frac{1}{2}$, $\frac{1}{4}$, $-\frac{3}{8}$
_____ **H.** prime numbers	**8.** $2\frac{1}{2}$, $3\frac{1}{4}$, $5\frac{7}{8}$
_____ **I.** composite numbers	**9.** $\frac{3}{4}$ (originally $\frac{6}{8}$), $\frac{1}{2}$ (originally $\frac{6}{12}$)
_____ **J.** odd numbers	**10.** 1

A:	**B:**	**C:**
D:	**E:**	**F:**
G:	**H:**	**I:**

Magic Number:

_____

Base *fin-, finit-*

fin-, finit- = "end," "term," "limit"

Standards

Uses a variety of strategies to extend reading vocabulary

Uses common, grade-appropriate Greek or Latin affixes and roots as clues to the meaning of a word

Materials

- *About the Root: Numbers that Have Limits* (page 46)

- *About the Root: Finite Sets* (page 47)

- *About the Root: Infinity* (page 48)

- *Divide and Conquer: Words Associated with End, Term, or Limit* (page 49)

- *Making Connections: Fill in the Blank* (page 50)

Teacher Preparation

- Read and review the background information about the base *fin-, finit-* on page 45 to familiarize yourself with words associated with "end," "term," or "limit."

- Read and review the glossary of the base found on the Digital Resource CD (filename: rootsglossary.pdf) for additional support.

Guided Practice

About the Root

1. Distribute copies of pages 46, 47, and/or 48 to students.

2. Write *fin-, finit-* = "end," "term," "limit" on the board. Discuss this base with the students.

3. Ask students to read the passages and answer the questions alone or with a partner. You may want to conclude with whole-class discussion.

Divide and Conquer

4. Distribute copies of *Divide and Conquer: Words Associated with End, Term, or Limit* (page 49). As you guide students through the activity page, use questions like these to generate discussion about each of the words:

   - Where is the meaning of "end," "term," or "limit" in the word _____?

   - Where might you see the word _____?

   - Can you think of an example of _____?

Base *fin-, finit-* (cont.)

Making Connections

5. Distribute copies of *Making Connections: Fill in the Blank* (page 50).

6. Ask students to skim the page before completing the activity.

7. To conclude this activity, ask pairs of students to rewrite a couple of sentences, maintaining meaning without using the underlined words. Share these, and ask other students whether meaning has been maintained.

Words with *fin-, finit-*

- ad infinitum
- confine
- define
- definite
- definition
- final
- finalize
- finance
- financial
- fine
- finery
- finesse
- finial
- finish
- finite
- indefinite
- infinite
- infinitesimal
- infinity
- quarterfinals
- refine
- refinements
- refinish
- semifinals
- superfine
- ultrafine

A list of words to print out for students can be found on the Digital Resource CD (filename: wordlists.pdf).

Teacher Background Information and Tips

Base *fin-, finit-* = "end," "term," "limit"

The Latin base *fin-, finit-* means "end," "term," "limit" and provides the base meaning of the mathematical concepts of *finite* and *infinite* numbers. Related mathematical terms built on this base include *infinitesimal*, meaning "endlessly small" (Latin negating prefix *in-* = "not"), *infinity*, *semifinals*, and *quarterfinals*.

Although the words *infinite* ("endlessly large" in extent or size) and *infinitesimal* ("endlessly small") are opposite in meaning, they both describe quantities which, since they have no end, remain immeasurable. We cannot measure *infinity*, and we cannot calculate amounts or sizes that are *infinitesimal* (Latin negative prefix *in-* = "not").

Although the related meanings of *end* and *limit* are easily understood, the word *term* is also associated with this Latin base. Think of a *bus terminal*, for example, which stands at the end of the line. A *terminal illness* results in the ultimate end of death. The word *definition* refers to putting down the terms of a word's meaning (Latin prefix *de-* = "down"). When we *finance* large purchases, we borrow money and agree with the lender on the *terms* of repayment.

Students may already know many everyday vocabulary and general academic words from this base, but they may not readily associate them with the base meaning of "end," "term," "limit." *Final examinations* are given at the end of the semester or school year (we also refer to school-year semesters as *terms*). When we *finalize* something, we put it in its *final* form, paying attention to end details. When we *finish* a project, we bring it to an end. Other *fin-, finit-* words which students may know as everyday words or as words from academic vocabulary are *define, definition, confine, definite,* and *indefinite*.

For a glossary of words built on these roots, see the Digital Resource CD (filename: rootsglossary.pdf).

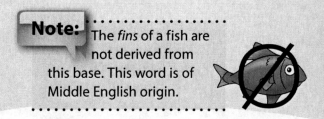

Note: The *fins* of a fish are not derived from this base. This word is of Middle English origin.

Name: _____ Date: _____

About the Root:
Numbers that Have Limits

Directions: Read the information below. Then answer the questions.

> The Latin base *fin-, finit-* means "end," "term," "limit." This base provides the core meaning of two important math concepts: *finite* and *infinite*. As you might guess, these words are opposites. *Finite* refers to something, such as a set of numbers, that has limits or can be counted. *Infinite*, on the other hand, has no limits and cannot be counted.

◎ The word *semifinal* is built on this base. How does this word's meaning include the idea of "end," "term," "limit"? (Keep in mind that *semi-* means "half" or "partial.")

_____

_____

_____

◎ You may take *finals* at the end of your math class. How does this word include the idea of "end," "term," "limit"?

_____

_____

_____

Name: _____ Date: _____

About the Root:
Finite Sets

Directions: Read the passage below. Then answer the question.

1 2 3 4 5 6 7 8 9 1 2 3 4 5 6 7 8 9

Think about the meaning of these two words: *set* and *finite*. A "set" is a collection of well-defined and distinct objects. "Finite" means capable of being counted.

Let's put these ideas together and think about numbers. A finite set is a group of numbers that can be counted. The group has a definite beginning and also a definite end. So, for example, the set of odd numbers that are greater than zero and less than ten is {1, 3, 5, 7, 9}. The items in this set are finite; they can be counted. Contrast this with an infinite set of odd numbers, also starting with 1. This second set would start the same, but it would never end.

The idea of finite sets is important in a branch of mathematics called *combinatorics*. This is the mathematical study of counting. Mathematicians have established properties of finite sets. For example, any subset of a finite set has fewer elements than the finite set. And also, any subset of a finite set is also finite. Using the example of odd numbers greater than zero and less than ten above, we could make a subset of numerals that have no curves: {1, 7}. Does this subset fit the properties? Does it have fewer elements than the original set? Is the subset also finite? Discuss these questions with a partner.

Look around your classroom. Develop two finite sets of things you can see. Write them down, and explain why you think they are finite sets.

_____

_____

_____

_____

_____

_____

Name: _____ Date: _____

About the Root:
Infinity

Directions: Read the passage below. Then answer the question.

In the *Toy Story* movies, Buzz Lightyear often says, "To infinity and beyond!" This is a silly saying, if you think about it. *Infinity* is a concept in many fields, such as mathematics, physics, and philosophy. It refers to a quantity without boundaries or endings. So since Buzz can't get to infinity—it has no ending—he certainly can't get beyond it!

In mathematics, infinity is often treated like a number. It is treated like something that can be used to count or measure things. It doesn't work like a number, however. Can you add, subtract, multiply, or divide using infinity? No.

Aristotle

Ancient Greek mathematicians and philosophers thought about infinity. Aristotle, for example, preferred to distinguish between "actual" infinity and "potential" infinity. He found the idea of actual infinity to be a paradox. How could something with no boundaries or endings actually be complete? Instead, Aristotle thought infinity should be described as "potential." Here is an example. Begin with the sequence {1, 2, 3}. One more number can always be added to the sequence. But the sequence can never be completed. There's no end to the process.

The mathematical symbol for infinity looks like the numeral 8 on its side (∞). Several branches of mathematics use the concept of infinity, including geometry, calculus, set theory, and even fractals.

Do you think actual infinity is possible? Explain your thinking.

_____

_____

_____

Name: _____ Date: _____

Divide and Conquer:
Words Associated with End, Term, or Limit

Directions: Use the Base/Prefix/Suffix Bank to help you identify the roots of the words below. *X* means the word does not contain that element. Write the letter from the Definition Bank for the correct word. The *-al* suffix makes two of the words adjectives.

Base/Prefix/Suffix Bank

con- = "with," "together"   *semi-* = "half," "partial"   *in-* = "not"

Definition Bank

A. immeasurably small

B. boundlessness; unlimited extent of time, space, or quantity

C. to limit or contain; to close off from others

D. having limits; capable of being counted or measured

E. a contest immediately preceding the last competition

Word	First Base/Prefix Means	Second Base/Suffix Means	Definition
1. infinity			
2. finite		X	
3. confine			
4. semifinal			
5. infinitesimal			

Name: _____ Date: _____

Making Connections:
Fill in the Blank

. . . .

Directions: Complete each sentence with the best word or phrase from the Word Bank. Then give examples of finite and infinite sets of numbers.

Word Bank			
ad infinitum	definitions	infinitely	final
confined	infinite	infinity	finite

1. All the numbers in a _____ set can be counted.

2. I can't call this particle "microscopic" since it is not visible even under a microscope. It is _____ small.

3. Do you think that some dictionary _____ are hard to understand?

4. The letter "pi" (π), which begins 3.14159… never ends. It is an _____ number.

5. I thought the speaker would never end. He was rambling on _____.

6. We keep our dog _____ in the backyard with a high fence and locked gates.

7. The human mind cannot fully comprehend _____.

8. The _____ word in the Word Bank will complete this sentence.

9. Give an example of a finite set of numbers: _____

10. Give an example of an infinite set of numbers: _____

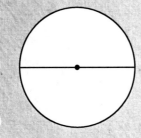

The Greek symbol pi denotes the ratio of a circle's circumference to its diameter. The numerical value of pi is infinite. It has no end point.

Base vers-, vert-

vers-, vert- = "turn," "change"

Standards

Uses conventions of spelling in written compositions

Determines the meaning of words and phrases as they are used in a text, including figurative, connotative, and technical meanings

Materials

- *About the Root: Turning and Changing in Math* (page 54)

- *About the Root: Transversals* (page 55)

- *About the Root: Converting Decimals, Percentages, and Fractions* (page 56)

- *Divide and Conquer: Words Associated with Change* (page 57)

- *Making Connections: Crossword Puzzle* (page 58)

Teacher Preparation

- Read and review the background information about the base *vers-, vert-* on page 53 to familiarize yourself with words associated with "change."

- Read and review the glossary of the base found on the Digital Resource CD (filename: rootsglossary.pdf) for additional support.

Guided Practice

About the Root

1. Distribute copies of pages 54, 55, and/or 56 to students.

2. Write *vers-, vert-* on the board. Tell students that this base means "turn" or "change."

3. Ask students to read the passages and answer the questions alone or with a partner. You may want to conclude with whole-class discussion.

Divide and Conquer

4. Distribute copies of *Divide and Conquer: Words Associated with Change* (page 57). As you guide students through the activity page, use questions like these to generate discussion about each of the words:

   - Where is the meaning of "turn" or "change" in the word _____?

   - Where might you see the word _____?

   - Can you think of an example of _____?

Base vers-, vert- (cont.)

Making Connections

5. Distribute copies of *Making Connections: Crossword Puzzle* (page 58).

6. Students can complete the crossword puzzle independently or with partners.

Words with vers-, vert-

adversary

adverse

adversity

advertise

averse

controversial

controversy

conversation

convert

diverse

inadvertent

inverse

invert

pervert

reverse

revert

subvert

transversal

traverse

universe

university

versatile

versatility

verse

vertebra

vertebrate

vertex

vertical

vertigo

A list of words to print out for students can be found on the Digital Resource CD (filename: wordlists.pdf).

Teacher Background Information and Tips

Base *vers-, vert-* = "turn," "change"

The Latin base *vers-, vert-*, meaning "turn," "change," appears in several important words from mathematical vocabulary. When we *convert* fractions into decimals, we change them. A *vertical* line is a horizontal line that has been turned upright. When we recite numbers in *reverse* order, we turn their sequence backwards. Adding and subtracting are *inverse* mathematical operations.

Although some of the mathematical terms built on this base can be challenging, these words lend themselves quite well to pictorial representation. You may wish to draw figures for students as you explain the words. For example, this sequence of *vers-, vert-* words can be illustrated by drawing lines and figures on the board. We start with an angle, identify its *vertex*, proceed to the *vertex* of a triangle, and finally intersect lines that create *vertical angles*. We follow with an explanation of how a *transversal* cuts across parallel lines and then proceed to explain direct and *inverse proportions*.

The Latin base *vers-, vert-* appears in a large number of everyday words, in general academic vocabulary, and in vocabulary from other content areas (e.g., *vertebrate*, *vertigo*, *adversity*).

For a glossary of words built on these roots, see the Digital Resource CD (filename: rootsglossary.pdf).

Name: _____   Date: _____

About the Root:
Turning and Changing in Math

Directions: Read the information below. Then answer the questions.

> The Latin base *vers-, vert-* means "turn," "change." This base appears in several important math words. For example, a *vertical* line is upright, "turned" from a horizontal to a standing position. When we *invert* a fraction, we "turn" it upside down: $\frac{4}{3}$ is the *inversion* of $\frac{3}{4}$.

◎ How does the idea of *converting* a decimal to a fraction include "turning" or "changing"?

_____

_____

_____

◎ Suppose you *reverse* this sequence: {1, 2, 3}. What is the reverse sequence? How does this include the idea of "turn" or "change"?

_____

_____

_____

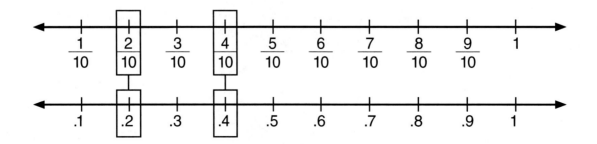

Name: _____ Date: _____

About the Root:
Transversals
. . . .

Directions: Read the passage below. Then answer the question.

Parallel lines run alongside each other without ever touching. (The Greek prefix *para-* means "alongside.") Think of railroad tracks or the rails (sides) of a ladder. We can extend them for miles, yet they will never intersect one another.

But we can draw a slanted line that cuts through two parallel lines. If we do, the slanted line is called a *transversal* or line that "turns" (*vers-*) "through or across" (*trans-*) another line. A transversal is a line that passes through two or more other lines in the same plane at different points.

When a transversal intersects parallel lines, it produces angles. If two parallel lines are transversed, eight angles result. If the transversal is perpendicular to the parallel lines, the resulting angles will be right angles. If the transversal is not perpendicular, oblique (not 90 degrees) angles will result.

How many angles result from a transversal of three parallel lines? _____

Draw a sketch to prove your answer.

Name: _____   Date: _____

About the Root:
Converting Decimals, Percentages, and Fractions

Directions: Read the passage below. Then answer the question.

Percentages and fractions represent parts of a whole. So do the numerals to the right of decimal points in numbers with decimals. Occasionally, we need to *convert* or change a fraction to a decimal or percentage, or the other way around. Here's how to do this.

Converting decimals to percentages or percentages to decimals is easy! If you are converting a percentage to a decimal, you simply move the decimal point two places to the left. For example, 27% is the same as 0.27. And 14.3% is the same as 0.143. To convert decimals to percentages, you move the decimal point two places to the right. For example, 0.88 is the same as 88% and 0.1645 is the same as 16.45%. Easy, right?

Converting percentages to fractions is also fairly easy. Percent means "out of a hundred," so the first step is to change the percentage to a fraction. 40% is 40 out of a hundred or, $\frac{40}{100}$. When you have a fraction, you can reduce the terms. So, $\frac{40}{100}$ can be reduced to $\frac{4}{10}$, and $\frac{4}{10}$ can be reduced to $\frac{2}{5}$.

Converting decimals to fractions is very similar. Recall that 40% is the same as .40, and .40 is the same as $\frac{40}{100}$. With this information, you can follow the rules above.

Select a decimal and convert it to a percentage. _____ = _____

Then convert it to a fraction. _____ = _____

Explain how you did this: _____

_____

_____

_____

Decimal	Percentage	Fraction
.25	25%	$\frac{1}{4}$
.75	75%	$\frac{3}{4}$

Name: _____ Date: _____

Divide and Conquer:
Words Associated with Change

Directions: Use the Base/Prefix/Suffix Bank to help you identify the roots of the words below. *X* means the word does not contain that element. Write the letter from the Definition Bank for the correct word. The *-al* suffix makes one of the words an adjective.

Base/Prefix/Suffix Bank

ad- = "to," "toward," "add to"   *in-* = "in," "on," "into"   *trans-* = "across," "change"
con- = "with," "together"   *re-* = "back," "again"

Definition Bank

A. change to make compatible with another group or system

B. turn back

C. opposite

D. a foe, rival, or opponent (someone you turn against)

E. a line that cuts across other lines

F. a line or structure turned upright

Word	First Base/Prefix Means	Second Base/Suffix Means	Definition
1. vertical		X	
2. convert			
3. inverse			
4. reverse			
5. transversal			
6. adversary			

Name: _____ Date: _____

Making Connections:
Crossword Puzzle

· ·

Directions: Use the words in the Word Bank to complete the crossword puzzle.

Word Bank

| angles | direct | perpendicular | transversal | vertex |
| conversion | inverse | square | triangle | vertical |

Across

4. The vertex of a _____ is the highest point from its base.

6. 3:6 :: 5:10 is an example of _____ proportion.

8. $\frac{1}{4}$ = 0.25 is an example of _____ of a fraction.

9. A _____ is a line that cuts across two or more parallel lines.

10. A _____ has four equal sides.

Down

1. Measuring the height of a triangle is _____ measurement.

2. Addition and subtraction are _____ operations.

3. A line cutting across two parallel lines at a right angle is called a _____ transversal.

5. The center letter in a 3-letter label of an angle is its _____.

7. Vertical _____ are always opposite to and equal to each other.

Bases *gon-* and *angl-, angul-*

gon-, angl-, angul- = "angle," "corner"

Standards

Uses a variety of strategies to extend reading vocabulary

By the end of the year, reads and comprehends literary nonfiction in the grades 6–8 text complexity band proficiently, with scaffolding as needed at the high end of the range

Materials

- *About the Root: Angles and Corners* (page 62)
- *About the Root: Polygons* (page 63)
- *About the Root: Triangles* (page 64)
- *Divide and Conquer: Words Associated with Angle and Corner* (page 65)
- *Making Connections: Riddles* (page 66)

Teacher Preparation

- Read and review the background information about the bases *gon-* and *angl-, angul-* on page 61 to familiarize yourself with words associated with "angle" and "corner."

- Read and review the glossary of the bases found on the Digital Resource CD (filename: rootsglossary.pdf) for additional support.

Guided Practice

About the Root

1. Distribute copies of pages 62, 63, and/or 64 to students.

2. Write *gon-* and *angl-, angul-* = "angle," "corner" on the board. Ask students to complete the first section on page 62. After a few minutes, invite sharing.

3. Ask pairs of students to read the rest of the passages and answer the questions. You may want to conclude with whole-class discussion. Students could brainstorm words containing the roots, for example, and you could post these in the classroom.

Divide and Conquer

4. Distribute copies of *Divide and Conquer: Words Associated with Angle and Corner* (page 65). As you guide students through the activity page, use questions like these to generate discussion about each of the words:

   - Where is the meaning of "angle" or "corner" in the word _____?
   - Where might you see the word _____?
   - Can you think of an example of _____?

Bases gon- and angl-, angul- (cont.)

Making Connections

5. Distribute copies of *Making Connections: Riddles* (page 66).

6. You may wish to write a riddle together with students. You might conclude with a discussion that focuses on root meaning.

Words with gon- and angl-, angul-

anchor

angle

angular

ankle

decagon

diagonal

dodecagon

equiangular

heptagon

hexagon

hexagonal

nonagon

octagon

octagonal

pentagon

polygon

polygonal

quadrangle

quadrangular

rectangle

rectangular

triangle

triangular

trigonometric

trigonometry

A list of words to print out for students can be found on the Digital Resource CD (filename: wordlists.pdf).

Teacher Background Information and Tips

Bases *gon-* and *angl-*, *angul-* = "angle," "corner"

The Greek base *gon-* and Latin base *angl-*, *angul-*, meaning "angle," "corner," appear in many words from geometry. In the original ancient languages, even before the development of geometry, these bases meant "bend," generating such non-math words as *ankle* (the joint at which the leg and foot meet, creating an *angular* bend) and *anchor* (originally, a bent piece of hooked metal dropped to the bottom of the sea to dig into the sand and stabilize the boat). The original meaning of "bend," "bent" can be helpful to students in visualizing an *angle:* an *angle* is created by two lines that intersect and form a corner at the *vertex* (see Unit I, Lesson 5), the "turning point" at which the line "bends."

The concept of an *angle* as a bent line can be illustrated by drawing a *right angle*. Without lifting pencil from paper (or marker from board), draw a vertical line (from top down) and then bend it at 90 degrees into a horizontal line. By drawing students' attention to the "bent corner," you can focus their attention on the *angle* itself. When we name *angles*, such as ∠ ABC, the center letter always identifies the *vertex*, or "turning point" of the two rays that bend at this spot.

When studying *angles*, students often learn the *classifications of angles*. Angles are classified in terms of 90 degrees, 180 degrees, and their variance from these measurements. Because a *polygon*, by definition, contains many sides and angles, students studying *angles* and *polygons* often learn the terminology of angles as they relate to one another.

This mnemonic may help students distinguish *complementary* from *supplementary* angles. Both *supplementary* and *straight* begin with the letter *s*. *Supplementary* angles combine to form a *straight* angle (the 180 degrees that constitute a *straight* line). Both *corner* and *complementary* begin with the letter *c*. *Complementary* angles combine to form the *corner* of a right angle.

For a glossary of words built on these roots, see the Digital Resource CD (filename: rootsglossary.pdf).

Name: _____ Date: _____

About the Root:
Angles and Corners

Directions: Read the information below. Then answer the questions.

> The bases *gon-* and *angl-*, *angul-* mean "angle," "corner." These bases appear in many words from geometry. You may already know, for example, such words as *polygon* and *hexagon*. Because a *hexagon* contains six angles, it also contains six sides. In general, a *polygon* has as many sides as it has *angles*. A geometric figure that consists of straight sides and *angles* always has an *angular* shape.

◎ *Poly-* means "many." What is a *polygon*? Give an example of a polygon, and then write how you know it is one.

_____

_____

_____

◎ *Octa(o)-* means "eight." How many corners does an *octagonal* figure have?

_____

◎ On many college campuses, buildings are arranged around an open, grassy area called a *quadrangle*. How many corners and sides would you expect to find in a *quadrangle* flanked by classroom buildings?

_____

_____

Name: _____ Date: _____

About the Root:
Polygons
. . . .

Directions: Read the passage below. Then answer the questions.

Polygons have many corners. They are flat, two-dimensional figures. They have been studied since ancient times. The word *polygon* is a generic term. It refers to any two-dimensional figure that has many sides or corners. A root that means a number is added to *-gon* to name a specific polygon. For example:

◎ *Penta-* means "five," so a *pentagon* has five corners.

◎ *Hexa-* means "six," so a *hexagon* has six corners.

◎ *Hepta-* means "seven," so a *heptagon* has seven corners.

◎ *Octa-* means "eight," so an *octagon* has eight corners.

> Regardless of the number of corners, all polygons share some characteristics. They are all formed from straight lines called *segments* or *edges*. The segments are linked together to form a closed chain. A vertex (plural: vertices) is the point where two segments meet. The line segments or rays that extend from vertices form angles; all polygons have angles.
>
> Polygons also have differences aside from their numbers of corners. For example, some polygons are simple, meaning that their segments do not intersect, except at their corners. Others, like stars, are complex with segments that do intersect. Some polygons are cyclic. This means that their corners could be located on a circle.

◎ Is a square a simple polygon or a complex polygon? Why?

_____

_____

◎ Is a square a cyclic polygon? Why?

_____

_____

Name: _____   Date: _____

About the Root:
Triangles
. . . .

Directions: Read the passage below. Then answer the questions on a separate sheet of paper.

A *triangle* is a two-dimensional polygon. Along with circles and rectangles, triangles are considered basic shapes. Triangles have three sides, sometimes called edges or segments. The sides are closed. They also have three angles or corners, also called *vertices*. Euclid described the basic facts and properties of triangles in 300 B.C.

The names of triangles depend on their shapes. Either the length of the sides or the size of the inside angles determines the type of triangle. For example, an equilateral triangle has three equal sides. *Equi-* means "equal" and *later-* means "side," so this is an easy one to remember. An *isosceles* triangle has at least two equal sides. If you know about *isobars* on weather maps, which connect places with equal atmospheric pressure, this may help you remember *isosceles*. (*Iso-* means "equal," and Greek *scel-* means "leg," "ankle," referring to the leglike sides of a triangle.) *Scalene* triangles have uneven sides.

Triangles can also be labeled according to their angles. The inside angles of a triangle always equal 180 degrees. An *equiangular* triangle has, as you might guess, equal angles. Each angle is 60 degrees. A *right triangle* has one 90 degree angle. *Acute* triangles have angles that are less than 90 degrees. *Obtuse* triangles have an angle greater than 90 degrees. Remembering that *A* comes before *O* in the alphabet may help you remember that acute triangles have smaller angles than obtuse triangles.

◎ Is an equilateral triangle also an isosceles triangle? How do you know?

◎ Could an obtuse triangle also be a right triangle? How do you know?

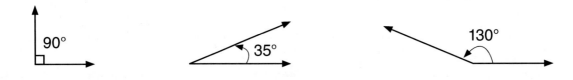

90°   35°   130°

Name: _____ Date: _____

Divide and Conquer:

Words Associated with Angle and Corner

Directions: Use the Base/Prefix/Suffix Bank to help you identify the roots of the words below. Write the letter from the Definition Bank for the correct word. The *-al* suffix makes three of the words adjectives.

Base/Prefix/Suffix Bank

dia- = "through," "across"   *oct(a)-* = "eight"   *rect-* = "right"
hex(a)- = "six"   *quadr-* = "four"

Definition Bank

A. a polygon with four angles of 90 degrees each

B. having six sides or angles

C. any four-sided polygon

D. having eight sides or angles

E. a line cutting across a polygon and connecting two nonadjacent angles

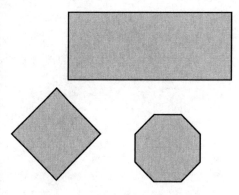

Word	First Base/Prefix Means	Second Base/Suffix Means	Definition
1. quadrangle			
2. diagonal			
3. rectangle			
4. octagonal			
5. hexagonal			

Name: _____ Date: _____

Making Connections:
Riddles

· ·

Directions: Make riddles for two of the terms in the Word Bank. Leave the last line blank. Then give your riddles to a classmate to solve. If you would like to create more riddles, use a separate sheet of paper.

Example:

I am a figure with many angles.

I have five letters; three are vowels.

The top of a child's wagon is my shape.

The top of a pizza box is my shape.

What am I?

Answer: a square

Word Bank

polygon	complex polygon	triangle
simple polygon	rectangle	term

1. _____

_____

_____

_____

_____

_____

2. _____

_____

_____

_____

_____

_____

Base *later-*

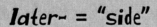

later- = "side"

Standards

Uses a variety of strategies to extend reading vocabulary

Uses common, grade-appropriate Greek or Latin affixes and roots as clues to the meaning of a word

Materials

- *About the Root: Side to Side* (page 70)

- *About the Root: Let's Go Fly a Kite!* (page 71)

- *About the Root: Polygons and Quadrilaterals* (page 72)

- *Divide and Conquer: Words Associated with Sides* (page 73)

- *Making Connections: Name that Quadrilateral!* (page 74)

Teacher Preparation

- Read and review the background information about the base *later-* on page 69 to familiarize yourself with words associated with "sides."

- Read and review the glossary of the base found on the Digital Resource CD (filename: rootsglossary.pdf) for additional support.

Guided Practice

About the Root

1. Distribute copies of pages 70, 71, and/or 72 to students.

2. Write *later-* = "side" on the board. Tell students that this base is the focus of the next few lessons. Explain that this base sounds like the word *ladder* and that they should not confuse it with the actual word *later*.

3. Ask students to read the passages and answer the questions. You may want to conclude with whole-class discussion, especially on the second passage *Let's Go Fly a Kite!*

Base *later-* (cont.)

Divide and Conquer

4. Distribute copies of *Divide and Conquer: Words Associated with Sides* (page 73). As you guide students through the activity page, use questions like these to generate discussion about each of the words:

- Where is the meaning of "side" in the word _____?

- Where might you see the word _____?

- Can you think of an example of _____?

Making Connections

5. Distribute copies of *Making Connections: Name that Quadrilateral!* (page 74).

6. Ask students to read all of the definitions before completing the activity sheet.

7. You might conclude with a discussion that focuses on root meaning. You may also want students to share their responses to the last two questions with one another.

Words with *later-*

bilateral
collateral
equilateral
lateral
multilateral
quadrilateral
trilateral
unilateral

A list of words to print out for students can be found on the Digital Resource CD (filename: wordlists.pdf).

Teacher Background Information and Tips

Base *later-* = "side"

The Latin base *later-*, meaning "side," appears in words from geometry describing *polygons*. Students may already know this base from sports: a football player makes a *lateral pass* by throwing the ball "sideways" and not directly forward. In geometry, this base always refers to the sides of a polygon.

Whereas the bases *gon-* and *angl-, angul-* emphasize the "angles" of a *polygon* (see previous lesson), words based on Latin *later-* emphasize the number of sides of a geometrical figure and the relationship between those sides. A *polygon* (a "many-angled" figure) is therefore also *multilateral* ("many sided"). The word *quadrangle* draws attention to the "four angles" of a square, a rectangle, a trapezoid, a parallelogram, or a rhombus, but the word *quadrilateral* draws attention to the fact that all these figures have "four sides." All *quadrilaterals* include four angles, which together add up to 360 degrees.

For a glossary of words built on this root, see the Digital Resource CD (filename: rootsglossary.pdf).

Name: _____ Date: _____

About the Root:
Side to Side
· ·

Directions: Read the information below. Then answer the questions.

> The Latin base *later-* means "side." *Polygons* have many corners; they also have many sides. In geometry, *later-* always refers to the sides of a polygon. All polygons are *multilateral* figures. When we want to indicate how many sides a particular polygon has, we simply attach the appropriate numerical prefix to the base *later-* (a *trilateral* polygon has three sides). In an *equilateral* polygon, all sides are of equal length.

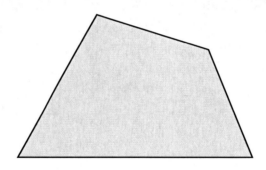

◎ Where is a *lateral* pass in football thrown—in front of, in back of, or to the side of the quarterback? How do you know?

_____

_____

_____

◎ *Quadr(i)-* means "four." How many sides does a *quadrilateral* have? _____

◎ What is another name for a *trilateral* figure? _____

Name: _____ Date: _____

About the Root:
Let's Go Fly a Kite!

Directions: Read the passage below. Then answer the question.

Think about the shape of an ordinary kite, the kind you might fly on a windy day. It has four sides, so it is a *quadrilateral*. It has pairs of sides that are the same length. But it's not like a parallelogram, where sides of equal length are across from (parallel to) each other. Instead, the pairs with equal sides are adjacent (next) to each other. The positioning of the equal sides is what gives kites their distinctive shape.

If you turn a toy kite over, you will see two small, round pieces of wood. One stretches from the top to the bottom, and the other stretches from side to side. In geometry, these are called the *diagonals* of the kite. They bisect and are at right angles to each other. Moreover, kites have an axis of symmetry along one of their diagonals. If you fold a kite on the long diagonal, the two halves will be triangles of the same shape.

Geometric kites are named for the kites we fly in the wind. And these toy kites are named after the bird, which is a raptor or bird of prey that spends a great deal of time just soaring through the air. The next time you fly a kite, think of all the geometry you know about it!

Draw a kite. Label the pairs of equal sides and the diagonals.

Name: _____   Date: _____

About the Root:
Polygons and Quadrilaterals

Directions: Read the passage below. Then answer the question.

What is a polygon? *Poly-* means "many." *Gon-* means "corner" or "angle." Thus, a polygon is a geometric shape consisting of at least three corners or angles. Triangles, squares, octagons—all of these (and more) are polygons.

Quadrilaterals are a group, or subset, of all polygons. Quadrilaterals have four sides and four vertices, or corners. They can be simple, with no intersecting lines, or complex, with lines that intersect. They are sometimes called *quadrangles*, meaning four angles. This term is comparable to triangles, meaning three angles.

There are several types of simple quadrilaterals. A parallelogram has two sets of parallel sides. Squares, rectangles, oblongs, and rhombuses are parallelograms. Not all quadrilaterals are parallelograms, however. Kites and trapezoids both have four sides, but do not have two sets of parallel sides.

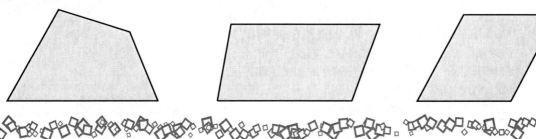

Put the following shape terms in order from broadest concept (1) to narrowest (6). Be prepared to explain your decisions.

◎ parallelogram _____   ◎ quadrilateral _____

◎ polygon _____   ◎ rectangle_____

◎ quadrangle _____   ◎ square _____

_____

_____

_____

_____

Name: _____ Date: _____

Divide and Conquer:
Words Associated with Sides

Directions: Use the Base/Prefix/Suffix Bank to help you identify the roots of the words below. *X* means the word does not contain the element. Write the letter from the Definition Bank for the correct word. The *-al* suffix makes one of the words an adjective.

Base/Prefix/Suffix Bank

bi- = "two," "both"   *equ(i)-* = "equal"
quadr(i)- = "four"   *tri-* = "three"

Definition Bank

A. consisting of three sides

B. consisting of four sides

C. sideways, occurring on the side, cast to the side

D. agreed upon by two sides or parties

E. having sides of equal length

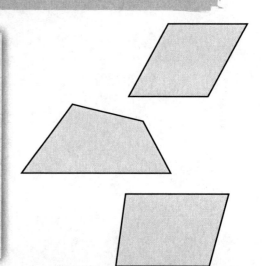

Word	First Base/Prefix Means	Second Base/Suffix Means	Definition
1. quadrilateral			
2. equilateral			
3. trilateral			
4. bilateral			
5. lateral		X	

Name: _____   Date: _____

Making Connections:
Name that Quadrilateral!

· ·

Directions: Match each math term in the first column with its description in the second column.

Math Term	**Description**
_____ **1.** rhombus	**A.** an equilateral parallelogram
_____ **2.** rectangle	**B.** an equilateral rectangle; also, a regular rectangle
_____ **3.** trapezoid	**C.** a quadrilateral with two pairs of parallel sides and with adjacent sides of unequal length (*adjacent* means "next to")
_____ **4.** parallelogram	
_____ **5.** square	**D.** a quadrilateral with four interior angles of 90 degrees each and with adjacent sides of unequal length
	E. a quadrilateral with only one pair of parallel sides

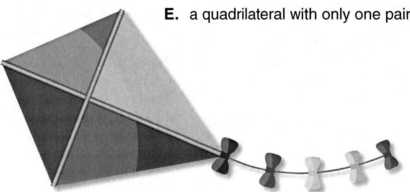

6. Here is a *parallelogram.* Indicate with a "tic" and a "double tic" the sides that are *congruent* ("congruent" means the same as one another).

7. Draw a *trilateral polygon.* What is another name for this figure?

_____

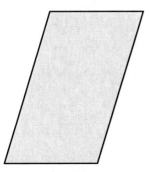

Base *seg-, sec-, sect-*

seg-, sec-, sect- = "cut"

Standards

Uses conventions of spelling in written compositions

Determines the meaning of words and phrases as they are used in a text, including figurative, connotative, and technical meanings

Materials

- *About the Root: Sections* (page 78)

- *About the Root: "Cutting" Circles* (page 79)

- *About the Root: Cross Sections* (page 80)

- *Divide and Conquer: Words Associated with Cutting* (page 81)

- *Making Connections: Fill in the Blank* (page 82)

Teacher Preparation

- Read and review the background information about the base *seg-, sec-, sect-* on page 77 to familiarize yourself with words associated with "cutting."

- Read and review the glossary of the base found on the Digital Resource CD (filename: rootsglossary.pdf) for additional support.

Guided Practice

About the Root

1. Distribute copies of pages 78, 79, and/or 80 to students.

2. Write *seg-, sec-, sect-* on the board. Tell students this base means "cut." Ask students to think of words they already know with this base. Invite sharing.

3. Ask students to read the passages and answer the questions alone or with a partner. You may want to conclude with whole-class discussion.

Divide and Conquer

4. Distribute copies of *Divide and Conquer: Words Associated with Cutting* (page 81). As you guide students through the activity page, use questions like these to generate discussion about each of the words:

   - Where is the meaning of "cut" in the word _____?

   - Where might you see the word _____?

   - Can you think of an example of _____?

Base seg-, sec-, sect- *(cont.)*

Making Connections

5. Distribute copies of *Making Connections: Fill in the Blank* (page 82).

6. Ask students to skim the page before completing the activity.

7. To conclude, ask partners to rewrite a couple of sentences. They should maintain meaning but not use the underlined word. Then have partners share these new sentences with one another. Each pair can evaluate the other's sentences as to clarity and whether meaning was maintained.

Words with seg-, sec-, sect-

bisect

bisector

dissect

insects

intersect

intersection

secant

sectional

section

sector

segment

trisect

vivisection

A list of words to print out for students can be found on the Digital Resource CD (filename: wordlists.pdf).

Spelling Hints:

We often hear the word *sector* applied to various *segments* of society. Such phrases as *private sector, public sector, economic sector,* and *business sector* refer to statistics that are illustrated in pie charts. These charts begin with a circle, indicating the original whole, which is then divided or cut into *sectors* that indicate percentages of the whole.

Teacher Background Information and Tips

Base *seg-, sec-, sect-* = "cut"

The Latin base *seg-, sec-, sect-*, which means "cut," generates important words from geometry. Students may already know words built on this base, although they may not associate them with the base meaning of "cut." When we peel an orange, for example, we observe that it divides naturally into *sections* that allow us to cut it apart without using a knife. A *sectional* sofa consists of one piece "cut" into individual parts or pieces of furniture. Roads and streets cut across each other at *intersections*. *Insects* were given their name because their bodies appear as if they have been cut into multiple *sections*.

In geometry, the Latin base *seg-, sec-, sect-* refers to a smaller portion that has been cut from a larger and original whole. This base appears in terms and phrases from the study of lines, circles, angles, and figures from both plane and solid geometry.

For a glossary of words built on these roots, see the Digital Resource CD (filename: rootsglossary.pdf).

Name: _____ Date: _____

About the Root:
Sections

. . . .

Directions: Read the information below. Then answer the questions.

> The Latin base *seg-, sec-, sect-* means "cut." This base is part of several important words from geometry. It is also part of general vocabulary words. You may be familiar, for example, with the *sections* of an orange that you find when you "cut" into it. In biology laboratories, students often *dissect* small animals by "cutting" them apart. Although a line is infinite in length, a line *segment* is finite and measurable. When so many students sign up for a class that they cannot fit into a single classroom, the principal may cut the oversized class into two smaller *sections.*

◎ The word *section* is built on this base. How do the sections of an orange, for example, bring to mind "cut"?

_____

_____

◎ Describe an *intersection* of lines using the word *cut.*

_____

_____

◎ *Bi-* means "two." How many lines would you need to *bisect* a circle?

_____

_____

◎ How would you go about cutting a three-foot long board into four equal *segments?*

_____

_____

Name: _____ Date: _____

About the Root:
"Cutting" Circles

Directions: Read the passage below. Then answer the question.

A circle is a basic two-dimensional shape. Circles are defined by points in a plane that are a given distance from a single point at the center. Circles are closed curves. And circles can be "cut" by lines. Each of these "cuts" or lines has a different name:

◎ A straight line from the center of the circle to any point on its edge is the *radius*.

◎ A straight line with end points on the circle is a *chord*.

◎ The *diameter* is a special type of chord. A diameter goes through the center and straight across a circle. A diameter *bisects* the circle. It turns the circle into two equal segments.

◎ If a chord extends beyond the perimeter of a circle, it is called a *secant*.

Which of the cuts above would be useful if the circle in question were a pizza? Explain your answer.

_____

_____

_____

_____

_____

_____

_____

Name: _____ Date: _____

About the Root:
Cross Sections

Directions: Read the passage below. Then answer the question.

In geometry, *cross sections* are intersections. The cross section of a two-dimensional figure is a line. The cross section of a three-dimensional figure is a plane. In either case, cross sections make slices of the figure.

Cross sections are useful in several professions. Architects use them to develop floor plans. A floor plan is a view of a three-dimensional object, such as a room, from the perspective of a horizontal plane through it. The cross section of a room, for example, may show the walls and floor but not the ceiling.

Cross sections are also frequently used in technical drawings. They are used to show the internal workings of three-dimensional objects. These drawings usually have different kinds of cross hatches (like tic-tac-toe grids) to show different materials within the object.

Cross sections are used in medicine as well. Computerized axial tomography creates cross sections. Using this process, the computer can construct or create cross sections of internal organs or bones. This is useful for diagnosis.

perpendicular bisector

Explain how cross sections of internal organs or bones might help doctors diagnose a patient's illness.

_____

_____

_____

_____

_____

Name: _____ Date: _____

Divide and Conquer:
Words Associated with Cutting

Directions: Use the Base/Prefix/Suffix Bank to help you identify the roots of the words below. *X* means the word does not contain that element. Write the letter from the Definition Bank for the correct word.

Base/Prefix/Suffix Bank

bi- = "two"   *inter-* = "between," "among"

dis- = "apart," "in different directions"   *tri-* = "three"

Definition Bank

A. cut apart; analyze

B. divide into two halves

C. cross or cut across

D. a line cutting through a circle

E. to cut into three equal portions

Word	First Base/Prefix Means	Second Base/Suffix Means	Definition
1. bisect			
2. secant		X	
3. trisect			
4. intersect			
5. dissect			

Name: _____ Date: _____

Making Connections:
Fill in the Blank

Directions: Complete each sentence with the best word from the Word Bank.

Word Bank

bisected	intersect	insects	sections	segment
dissecting	intersection	section	sector	trisect

Sentences

1. You will turn right at the _____ of Main Street and Water Street.

2. Can you divide an orange into its natural _____ without having the juice squirt?

3. We will need to _____ this pizza with precision if all three of us are to get equal portions.

4. The construction workers are now laying the final _____ of the train tracks.

5. After serving 20 years in Congress, the senator left to work in the private _____.

6. She was so fascinated by _____ that she decided to become an entomologist.

7. If two lines are not parallel, they will eventually _____.

8. I _____ a right angle and produced two angles of 45 degrees.

9. The very thought of _____ a frog makes me squirm!

10. The doctor performed a Cesarean _____ to deliver the baby.

11. How many angles are in a *trisected* right angle, and how many degrees are in each one?

    _____

A————————•————————————•————————B

Although the line extends into infinity, the line segment AB in this diagram has a finite measurement.

Bases *iso-* and *equ(i)-*, *equat-*

iso-, equ(i)-, equat- = "equal"

Standards

Uses a variety of strategies to extend reading vocabulary

By the end of the year, reads and comprehends literary nonfiction in the grades 6–8 text complexity band proficiently, with scaffolding as needed at the high end of the range

Materials

- *About the Root: Equal* (page 86)

- *About the Root: Euclidian Plane Isometry* (page 87)

- *About the Root: Equilateral Triangles* (page 88)

- *Divide and Conquer: Words Associated with Equality* (page 89)

- *Making Connections: Fill in the Blank* (page 90)

Teacher Preparation

- Read and review the background information about the bases *iso-* and *equ(i)-, equat-* on page 85 to familiarize yourself with words associated with "equality."

- Read and review the glossary of the bases found on the Digital Resource CD (filename: rootsglossary.pdf) for additional support.

Guided Practice

About the Root

1. Distribute copies of pages 86, 87, and/or 88 to students.

2. Write *iso-* and *equ(i)-, equat-* on the board. Tell students that these bases mean "equal." Have students think about words they already know with these bases.

3. Ask partners to read and discuss the passages. They should answer the questions together. You may want to conclude with whole-class discussion.

Divide and Conquer

4. Distribute copies of *Divide and Conquer: Words Associated with Equality* (page 89). As you guide students through the activity page, use questions like these to generate discussion about each of the words:

   - Where is the meaning of "equal" in the word _____?

   - Where might you see the word _____?

   - Can you think of an example of _____?

Bases *iso-* and *equ(i)-*, *equat-* *(cont.)*

Making Connections

5. Distribute copies of *Making Connections: Fill in the Blank* (page 90).

6. Ask students to skim the page before completing the activity.

7. To conclude this activity, you might ask pairs of students to define some of the words in the Word Bank. Be sure students use "equal" in their definitions. Students may want to share their definitions with one another.

Words with *iso-* and *equ(i)-*, *equat-*

isogonic

isometric

isometry

isosceles

equal

equality

equate

equation

equator

equiangular

equidistant

equilateral

equilibrium

equinox

equivalent

A list of words to print out for students can be found on the Digital Resource CD (filename: wordlists.pdf).

Teacher Background Information and Tips

Bases *iso-* and *equ(i)-*, *equat-* = "equal"

The Greek base *iso-* and the Latin base *equ(i)-*, *equat-*, meaning "equal," appear in words from general math and from geometry. Students will quickly recognize the Latin base from such everyday words as *equal* and *equality*. The mathematical term, *properties of equality*, is explained below.

The word *equator* is of special interest to math students. In order to pinpoint locations on the globe of Earth, geographers employ a grid system of coordinates. The horizontal axis of this coordinate plane is called the *equator* because it divides the sphere of the globe into two equal hemispheres, the Northern Hemisphere and the Southern Hemisphere. The *equator* is the line that *equates* the two hemispheres. Degrees of latitude indicate the distance of a point as north or south of the equator. The vertical axis of this coordinate plane is the prime meridian. We measure distances east or west of the prime meridian as degrees of longitude.

While learning the Latin base *equ(i)-*, *equat-*, students can review how to compute:

* *equivalent fractions*
* *equivalent decimals*
* *equilateral polygons* (also called *regular polygons*)
* *balancing an equation*
* *properties of equality*

For example, *properties of equality* are *equal* amounts that are added to or subtracted from each side of an *equation*. If $a = b$, then $a + 3 = b + 3$, and so on. In order to compute the value of x in the *equation*, $x + 17 = 25$, we would use a *subtraction property of equality* of 17, as follows: $x + 17 - 17 = 25 - 17; x = 8$.

Name: _____ Date: _____

About the Root:
Equal

. . . .

Directions: Read the information below. Then answer the questions.

The Greek base *iso-* and the Latin base *equ(i)-*, *equat-*, mean "equal." These bases appear in words from general math and from geometry. They also appear in general vocabulary words. *Equal* and *equality* contain the base e*qu(i)-*. For example, the *equator* is the line around the globe of Earth that divides it into two "equal" halves: the Northern and the Southern Hemispheres. When we convert fractions into *equivalent* decimals, we aim for numbers of "equal" value; thus, 0.5 and $\frac{1}{2}$ are *equivalent* quantities. We can call a square an *equilateral* rectangle because all four of its sides are of "equal" length.

We find the Greek base *iso-* in the term *isosceles* triangle. In an *isosceles* triangle, two of three sides are of "equal" length. When people perform *isometric* exercises, they apply "equal" force to their muscle groups.

◎ How does a mathematical *equation* reflect the idea of "equal"?

_____

_____

_____

◎ Envision an *equilateral* triangle. Since all three of its sides are of "equal" length, is an *equilateral* triangle also *equiangular*? Explain.

_____

_____

_____

Name: _____ Date: _____

About the Root:
Euclidian Plane Isometry

Directions: Read the passage below. Then answer the question.

In geometry, a plane is a flat surface that is infinitely large and has no thickness. In other words, its length and width cannot be measured, since it has no edges. Its thickness cannot be measured since it is so thin that it has no thickness at all. Despite its "unreal" status, Euclidian plane *isometry* is easy to understand. It is any way of transforming a plane without deforming it.

Although it is not a true plane, imagine a large sheet of transparent plastic with your name written on it. We can use this to understand isometry. You could slide the plastic sheet to the right or left or up or down. This type of isometry is called *translation*. You could also rotate the plastic, called *rotation*. You could turn the whole sheet over, in which case your name would be upside down, a process called *reflection*. If you turn it backward as well, this is called *glide reflection*. Your name would be upside down and backwards.

The four types of isometry described above transform the plastic without deforming it. But there are some things you cannot do—cutting, folding, or melting the plastic, for example. These are not isometries.

Why are cutting, folding, and melting not considered isometries?

_____

_____

_____

_____

_____

_____

_____

Name: _____ Date: _____

Equilateral Triangles

Directions: Read the passage below. Then answer the question.

"Divide and conquer" the word *equilateral*. *Equi-* means "equal" and *lat-* means "side." From this, can you figure out what an *equilateral* triangle is? It's a triangle with equal sides! Sometimes, these triangles are called *equiangular*. This is because the inside angles on any equilateral triangle are also equal. Each is 60 degrees.

Several geometry theorems apply to equilateral triangles. One is called *Napoleon's Theorem*. This theorem is named for Napoleon Bonaparte, the French leader from the 19th century. Bonaparte was an amateur mathematician. (William Rutherford, another amateur mathematician, may have discovered the theorem. He published a magazine article about it in 1825. We are not really certain who discovered the theorem. It's a mathematical mystery!)

Napoleon's Theorem has several parts. First, you can draw equilateral triangles on the sides of any other triangle. Second, these "side" triangles can go outward or inward from the original triangle. Third, you can find the centers of these new triangles. Finally, if you connect the centers, this will also form an equilateral triangle.

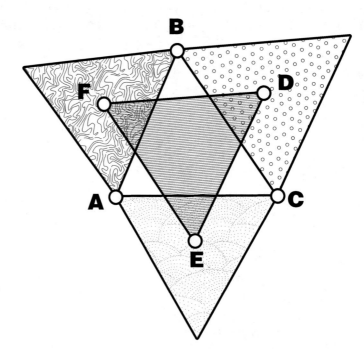

Locate the different triangles and discuss them with a partner.

Name: _____ Date: _____

Divide and Conquer:
Words Associated with Equality

Directions: Use the Base/Prefix/Suffix Bank to help you identify the roots of the words below. Write the letter from the Definition Bank for the correct word. The *-ar* and *-al* suffixes make two of the words adjectives.

Base/Prefix/Suffix Bank

angl-, angul- = "angle"	*later-* = "side"	*libr-* = "scale," "balance," "weight"
scel- = "ankle," "leg"	*val-* = "power," "strong"	

Definition Bank

A. having two or more equal or congruent sides (of a triangle)

B. having all sides of equal length (of any polygon)

C. state of balance

D. consisting of congruent angles

E. equal in value or amount

Word	First Base/Prefix Means	Second Base/Suffix Means	Definition
1. equilibrium			
2. equivalent			
3. isosceles			
4. equiangular			
5. equilateral			

Name: _____ Date: _____

Making Connections:
Fill in the Blank

Directions: Complete each sentence with the best word from the Word Bank.

Word Bank

| equation | equidistant | equinox | isometric | isosceles |
| equiangular | equilateral | equivalent | equal | |

Sentences

1. Every year, the vernal _____ falls on or around March 21 across the entire globe.

2. We traditionally use the term "square" to designate a particular polygon as an _____ rectangle.

3. The two legs of an _____ triangle are always congruent.

4. An equilateral triangle is also _____.

5. The fraction $\frac{3}{4}$ and the percentage of 75% are _____.

6. In the _____, $x + 15 = 22$, $x = 7$.

7. Many elderly people who cannot lift weights perform _____ exercises to maintain muscle tone.

8. The United States Declaration of Independence boldly declares, "All men are created _____."

9. Although my friend and I live at _____ points from school, it takes me longer to get there because of the heavy traffic.

10. Using the word *equal* in your answer, describe in your own words what it means to "balance an equation."

_____

_____

_____

Base tang-, tag-, tig-, tact-

tang-, tag-, tig-, tact- = "touch"

Standards

Uses conventions of spelling in written compositions

Uses common, grade-appropriate Greek or Latin affixes and roots as clues to the meaning of a word

Materials

- *About the Root: Touch* (page 94)
- *About the Root: Contingency Tables* (page 95)
- *About the Root: Tangents* (page 96)
- *Divide and Conquer: Words Associated with Touch* (page 97)
- *Making Connections: Magic Square* (page 98)

Teacher Preparation

- Read and review the background information about the base *tang-, tag-, tig-, tact-* on page 93 to familiarize yourself with words associated with "touch."

- Read and review the glossary of the base found on the Digital Resource CD (filename: rootsglossary.pdf) for additional support.

Guided Practice

About the Root

1. Distribute copies of pages 94, 95, and/or 96 to students.

2. Write *tang-, tag-, tig-, tact-* on the board. Tell students that this base, which has several spellings, means "touch." Students may complete the *About the Root* pages independently or with partners.

3. Conclude with whole-class discussion. You may wish to have students brainstorm a list of words with this base from the passages.

Divide and Conquer

4. Distribute copies of *Divide and Conquer: Words Associated with Touch* (page 97). As you guide students through the activity page, use questions like these to generate discussion about each of the words:

   - Where is the meaning of "touch" in the word _____?
   - Where might you see the word _____?
   - Can you think of an example of _____?

Base *tang-, tag-, tig-, tact-* (cont.)

Making Connections

5. Distribute copies of *Making Connections: Magic Square* (page 98).

6. Students may complete the Magic Square independently or with partners.

Words with *tang-, tag-, tig-, tact-*

contact

contagious

contiguous

contingency

intact

tactile

tangency

tangible

tangent

A list of words to print out for students can be found on the Digital Resource CD (filename: wordlists.pdf).

Teacher Background Information and Tips

Base *tang-, tag-, tig-, tact-* = "touch"

The Latin base *tang-, tag-, tig-, tact-* means "touch." It appears in words from everyday vocabulary, general academic vocabulary, and mathematical vocabulary. Students may already be using many words built on this base without realizing that they carry the base meaning of "touch." When we *contact* each other by phone, for example, we "get in touch" (Latin prefix *con-* = "with," "together"; literally, to get in "touch with"). We avoid touching people who carry a *contagious* illness, since germs can be transmitted *on contact* (i.e., "touching together"). A tornado may devastate many homes in an area but leave other houses whole and *intact* ("not touched").

In science, things that we can touch and feel are endowed with *tactile* properties, just as touch is our *tactile* sense. When we address sensitive subjects with a fine touch and with finess, we are *tactful.* In economics, *tangible* assets are real and "touchable," able to be assessed and appraised. In geography, students learn that the *contiguous* states of the United States exclude Hawaii and Alaska, which do not share *contiguous* borders with any other states.

For a glossary of words built on these roots, see the Digital Resource CD (filename: rootsglossary.pdf).

Name: _____ Date: _____

About the Root:
Touch

. . . .

Directions: Read the information below. Then answer the questions.

> The Latin base *tang-, tag-, tig-, tact-* means "touch." Words with this base are in everyday vocabulary, general academic vocabulary, and mathematical vocabulary. You probably already know words with this base. For example, when we *contact* our friends, we get in "touch" with them. If we have a *contagious* illness, we should avoid "touching" others so that we do not spread our germs.
>
> In math, geometric figures that "touch" each other are called *contiguous*. A line that "touches" a circle at only one point without intersecting it is called a *tangent*.

◎ Illinois and Indiana are *contiguous* states. Use "touch" to explain what *contiguous* means (**Hint:** *con-* means "with" or "together").

_____

_____

_____

◎ In this triangle, name two sides that are *contiguous*. Using the word *touch*, explain what *contiguous* means (**Hint:** The prefix *con-* = "with," "together").

_____

◎ One of these circles shows a *tangent,* and the other shows a diameter. Which is which? How do you know?

_____

_____

Name: _____   Date: _____

About the Root:
Contingency Tables

Directions: Read the passage below. Then answer the question.

Statistics is the study of data. Collecting, organizing, analyzing, and interpreting data are all parts of statistics. Researchers use statistics to answer questions about the natural world, human behavior, and many other issues. Researchers try to understand why things vary. Their data usually have something to do with variables.

After data about variables are gathered, a researcher must find a way to analyze the data. This process often involves organization. This is how contingency tables are used. *Contingency* tables are matrices that show the frequency and distribution of variables. Usually, these are categorical variables, which can be counted but not measured. Gender, people's names, and hair color are examples of categorical variables. The cells in a contingency table are organized so that they touch one another.

Here's an example: Suppose you have 30 people in your math class, 14 boys and 16 girls. You check people's eye colors—blue, brown, or green—and count how many boys and girls have each color of eyes. You could list all this information, but it would be hard to see patterns in the data. A contingency table makes patterns easier to see.

Gender	Blue	Brown	Green	Totals
Male	2	10	2	14
Female	3	9	4	16
Totals	5	19	6	30

Look at the contingency table above. Write two observations about the data in the table.

_____

_____

_____

_____

Name: _____ Date: _____

About the Root:
Tangents

Directions: Read the passage below. Then answer the question.

> A first grade teacher was introducing the concept of *rectangle* to his class. He was trying to help children see the rectangles in their lives. He pointed to classroom windows and the monitor on the classroom computer. Then, he asked the children, "What shape is your television set at home?" He expected the children to reply "rectangle," of course, but instead, children started talking about what they had watched on television over the weekend, where in their homes televisions were located, and so forth. The children went off on *tangents*, topics nearly unrelated to the main topic but "just touching" or sharing a single common point with it.
>
> This idea of single common point also applies to tangents in mathematics. In geometry, a tangent line or a tangent is a straight line that "just touches" a curve or a sphere. Similarly, a tangent plane is a plane that "just touches" a curved geometric figure. Circles can also be tangential to each other, if they "just touch" at a single point. Tangents do not overlap or cross the figures. They "just touch."

Draw a tangent to a circle. Then draw two circles that are tangent to each other. Write about how you decided what to draw.

_____

_____

_____

Name: _____   Date: _____

Divide and Conquer:
Words Associated with Touch

Directions: Use the Base/Prefix/Suffix Bank to help you identify the roots of the words below. *X* means the word does not contain that element. Write the letter from the Definition Bank for the correct word.

Base/Prefix/Suffix Bank

con- = "with," "together"   *in-* = "not"   *-ible* = "able"

Definition Bank

A. adjoined; adjacent; touching

B. real; material; able to be touched or grasped

C. connection; also, to get in touch with someone

D. a line which touches a circle at only one point

E. whole and untouched

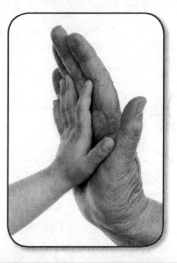

Word	First Base/Prefix Means	Second Base/Suffix Means	Definition
1. tangent		X	
2. contiguous			
3. intact			
4. contact			
5. tangible			

Name: _____ Date: _____

Making Connections:
Magic Square

. . . .

Directions: Match the definitions on the right with the words and phrases on the left. Put the numbers of your answers in the magic square. You can check your answers by adding each row and each column. Sums will be the same. **Note***: You will not use four of the definitions.*

Word/Phrase

_____ **A.** tangent line

_____ **B.** contiguous angles

_____ **C.** contiguous

_____ **D.** intact

_____ **E.** contact

_____ **F.** tangible

_____ **G.** tangent plane

_____ **H.** contingency tables

_____ **I.** contiguous sides

Definition

1. An _____ triangle has two equal sides.
2. We are fortunate that the terrible storm left our town _____.
3. A _____ is a line with end points on a circle.
4. The _____ of a circle is its perimeter.
5. In this square, sides C and D are _____.
6. Except for Alaska and Hawaii, the other 48 states are _____.
7. Statisticians may use _____ _____ to display data.
8. If you divided a right angle in half, the result would be two _____ of 45 degrees each.
9. Parallel lines never come into _____.
10. A _____ "just touches" a circle.
11. The number pi goes on to _____.
12. A _____ "just touches" a sphere.
13. A _____ object is real. It can be touched.

A:	B:	C:
D:	E:	F:
G:	H:	I:

Magic Number:

_____

Prefixes *peri-* and *circum-*

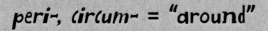

peri-, circum- = "around"

Standards

Uses a variety of strategies to extend reading vocabulary

Determines the meaning of words and phrases as they are used in a text, including figurative, connotative, and technical meanings

Materials

- *About the Root: Around the Edge* (page 102)

- *About the Root: Perimeter and Circumference* (page 103)

- *About the Root: Circles and Ellipses* (page 104)

- *Divide and Conquer: Words Associated with Around* (page 105)

- *Making Connections: Who/What Am I?* (page 106)

Teacher Preparation

- Read and review the background information about the prefixes *peri-* and *circum-* on page 101 to familiarize yourself with words associated with "around."

- Read and review the glossary of the prefixes found on the Digital Resource CD (filename: rootsglossary.pdf) for additional support.

Guided Practice

About the Root

1. Distribute copies of pages 102, 103, and/or 104 to students.

2. Write *peri-* and *circum-* on the board. Tell students that these bases have the same meaning, "around."

3. Ask students to read the passages and answer the questions alone or with a partner. You may want to conclude with whole-class discussion.

Divide and Conquer

4. Distribute copies of *Divide and Conquer: Words Associated with Around* (page 105). As you guide students through the activity page, use questions like these to generate discussion about each of the words:

   - Where is the meaning of "around" in the word _____?

   - Where might you see the word _____?

   - Can you think of an example of _____?

Prefixes *peri-* and *circum-* (cont.)

Making Connections

5. Distribute copies of *Making Connections: Who/What Am I?* (page 106).

6. Ask students to read all of the definitions before completing the activity sheet. You might conclude with a discussion that focuses on root meaning.

Words with *peri-* and *circum-*

circle
circular
circuit
circuitous
circulate
circulation
circulatory
circumambulate
circumference
circumlotion
circumnavigate
circumscribe
circumstances
circumvent
recirculate
semicircle
perigee
perihelion
perimeter
period
periodontist
peripheral
periphery
periscope
peristyle

A list of words to print out for students can be found on the Digital Resource CD (filename: wordlists.pdf).

Teacher Background Information and Tips

Prefixes *peri-* and *circum-* = "around"

The Greek prefix *peri-* and the Latin prefix *circum-* mean "around." These prefixes appear in many words from math. Latin *circum-* appears in math words describing circles, ovals, and arcs. Greek *peri-* appears in math words describing polygons and measurement of angles.

For example, the measurement around a circle is called the *circumference* (Latin *fer-* = "bear," "go"), but the measurement around a triangle, a rectangle, or any other polygon is called its *perimeter* (Greek *meter-* = "measure").

These prefixes appear in academic vocabulary words that some students may already know (e.g., *periscope, periphery*). Occasionally, Latin *circum-* is written as *circ(u)-* (without the final *m*), as in the words *circle, circular, circulate, circulatory,* and *circulation*. In these words, *circ(u)-* functions as a base, providing the word with its core meaning. In the words *semicircle* (Latin *semi-* = "half," "partial") and *recirculate* (Latin *re-* = "back," "again"), furthermore, prefixes attach to *circ(u)-*, which functions as the base.

For a glossary of words built on these roots, see the Digital Resource CD (filename: rootsglossary.pdf).

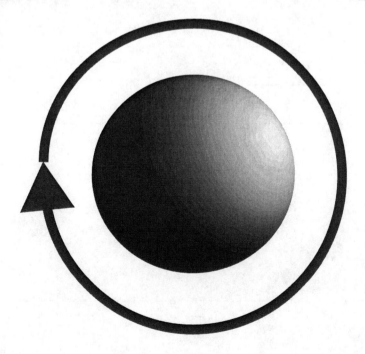

Name: _____ Date: _____

About the Root:
Around the Edge

Directions: Read the information below. Then answer the questions.

> In this unit, you will learn about pairs of Greek and Latin roots that have the same meaning. First, we focus on the Greek prefix *peri-* and the Latin prefix *circum-*. Both of these mean "around." These prefixes appear in many words from math. Latin *circum-* appears in math words describing circles, ovals, and arcs. Greek *peri-* appears in math words describing polygons and measurement of angles.

◎ How does the word *circumference* include the idea of "around"?

_____

_____

_____

◎ How does the word *perimeter* include the idea of "around"?

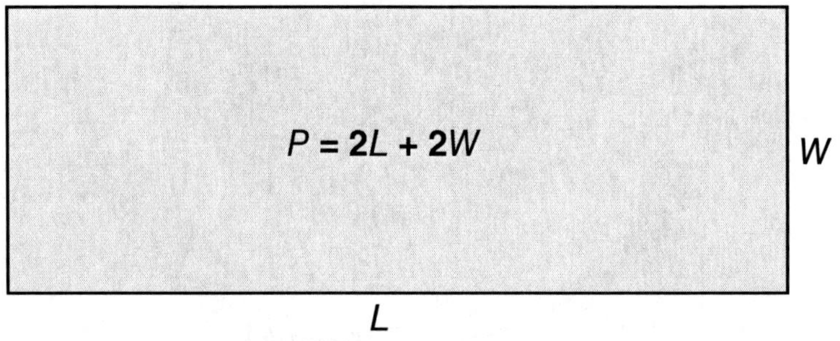

_____

_____

_____

$$P = 2L + 2W$$

W

L

Name: _____   Date: _____

About the Root:
Perimeter and Circumference

Directions: Read the passage below. Then answer the question.

The word *perimeter* comes from two Greek words. *Peri-* means "around," and *-meter* means "measure." From this, you can figure out that a *perimeter* is the measurement around a two-dimensional figure. You could also think of it as a path that surrounds a shape or the length of a boundary around a shape.

The formula for determining a perimeter depends on the shape. For triangles, perimeter = A + B + C, where these are lengths of the sides. For squares, perimeter = 4A, where A is the length of one side. And for rectangles, perimeter = 2 (L + W), where L is height and W is width. If you think about these equations, you will see that each describes a path for measuring around a figure.

The radius of a circle is the distance from its center to its edge. The diameter of a circle is the distance across it, or twice the radius. Do circles have perimeters? Yes, and they have a special name: *circumference*. But measuring them is a bit trickier, because circles do not have straight sides. To account for the curvy shape of circles, we use *pi*, a constant number that represents the ratio of any circle's circumference to its diameter. *Pi* is an infinite number, but we abbreviate it: 3.14159…. The perimeter or circumference of a circle is 2 *pi* R, where R is the radius, or *pi* D, where D is the diameter.

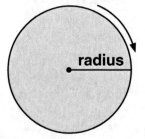

circumference

radius

circumference = 2 × π × radius

π = 3.14

Draw a triangle, a square, and a rectangle. Use the formulas in paragraph 2 above to label the sides of each figure.

Name: _____   Date: _____

About the Root:
Circles and Ellipses

Directions: Read the passage below. Then answer the question.

    Imagine that you could pull opposite ends of a *circle*. What would happen? The ends that you pulled would go out, and the other two ends of the circle would move closer together. So instead of something that looks like a hamburger bun (circle), if you pulled hard enough, you would have a shape like a hot-dog bun. This hot-dog-bun-shaped figure is called an *ellipse*.

    Ellipses can range from nearly *circular* to hardly circular. This is called their *eccentricity*. The shape of the ellipse is described by decimals. Decimals close to 1, such as .8 or .9, describe ellipses that are long and skinny. Decimals close to zero, such as .1 or .2, describe ellipses that are close to being circular.

    Earth's orbit around the sun is elliptical. Its eccentricity is 0.2. For this reason, once each year—every January—the distance from Earth to the sun is smallest. This is called the *perihelion* (*heli[o]-* means "sun" in Greek). And once each year—every July—the distance from Earth to the sun is greatest. This is called the *aphelion*. The difference between perihelion distance and aphelion distance is only 3 percent, but this is 4 million miles!

    Is Earth's orbit more like a hamburger bun or a hot dog bun? How do you know?

_____

_____

_____

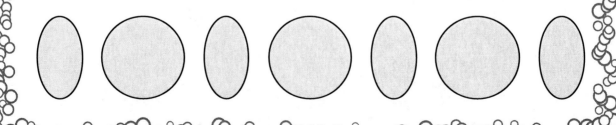

Name: _____ Date: _____

Divide and Conquer:
Words Associated with Around

Directions: Use the Base/Prefix/Suffix Bank to help you identify the roots of the words below. Write the letter from the Definition Bank for the correct word. The *-al* suffix makes one of the words an adjective.

Base/Prefix/Suffix Bank

fer- = "bear," "go"   *pher-* = "bear," "go"   *semi-* = "half," "partial"
meter- = "measure"   *scrib-* = "write," "draw"

Definition Bank

A. the measurement around a circle

B. to draw one circle or figure around another; to enclose within a circle

C. the measurement around the sides of a polygon

D. marginal; not central

E. a half-circle

Word	First Base/Prefix Means	Second Base/Suffix Means	Definition
1. perimeter			
2. semicircle			
3. circumference			
4. circumscribe			
5. peripheral			

Name: _____ Date: _____

Making Connections:
Who/What Am I?

Directions: Match each word or phrase in the first column with its speaker in the second column.

Word/Phrase   **Speaker**

_____ **1.** peripheral vision

_____ **2.** circumlocution

_____ **3.** circumscribed polygon

_____ **4.** angles

_____ **5.** perigee

_____ **6.** periodontist

_____ **7.** semicircle

_____ **8.** circumnavigation

_____ **9.** circuitous route

_____ **10.** peripheral concern

A. Portuguese explorer Ferdinand Magellan performed me when he sailed around the globe.

B. I am a marginal issue of no central importance.

C. I treat patients who have gum disease.

D. I am a triangle with a circle drawn inside.

E. I am the point in the moon's orbit where it is nearest to the Earth.

F. I am a roundabout way of speaking, often used by someone who beats around the bush and never gets to the point.

G. I measure 180 degrees.

H. If you divided a right angle in half, the result would be two _____ of 45 degrees each.

I. I am an indirect path, often traveling in circles.

J. I allow you to see outside the corner of your eye.

11. Use the word *peripheral*, *circumstances*, or *periodically* in a sentence.

_____

_____

Prefixes *dia-* and *per-*

dia- = "through," "across," "thorough"

per- = "through," "thorough"

Standards

Uses conventions of spelling in written compositions

By the end of the year, reads and comprehends literary nonfiction in the grades 6–8 text complexity band proficiently, with scaffolding as needed at the high end of the range

Materials

- *About the Root: Through and Across* (page 110)

- *About the Root: Estimating the Size of an Object* (page 111)

- *About the Root: From Math to Everyday Speech: Diameter* (page 112)

- *Divide and Conquer: Words Associated with Through, Across, or Thorough* (page 113)

- *Making Connections: Unscramble* (page 114)

Teacher Preparation

- Read and review the background information about the prefixes *dia-* and *per-* on page 109 to familiarize yourself with words associated with "through," "across," "thorough."

- Read and review the glossary of the prefixes found on the Digital Resource CD (filename: rootsglossary.pdf) for additional support.

Guided Practice

About the Root

1. Distribute copies of pages 110, 111, and/or 112 to students.

2. Write *dia-* = "through," "across," "thorough" and *per-* = "through," "thorough" on the board. Tell students that these roots are prefixes, which appear at the beginnings of words. Ask students to think of words they already know that contain these roots.

3. Ask pairs of students to read the passages and answer the questions. You may want to conclude with whole-class discussion.

Prefixes *dia-* and *per-* (cont.)

Divide and Conquer

4. Distribute copies of *Divide and Conquer: Words Associated with Through, Across, or Thorough* (page 113). As you guide students through the activity page, use questions like these to generate discussion about each of the words:

- Where is the meaning of "through," "across," or "thorough" in the word _____?

- Where might you see the word _____?

- Can you think of an example of _____?

Making Connections

5. Distribute copies of *Making Connections: Unscramble* (page 114).

6. Students can work independently or with partners. You might conclude by asking students to explain their responses. Focus this discussion on root meaning.

Words with *dia-* and *per-*

diabetes

diagnose

diagonal

diagram

dialect

dialogue

diameter

diametric

diaphanous

diaphragm

per

per annum

percent

percolate

perfect

perforate

permanent

permeate

perplex

perpendicular

perspective

perturb

A list of words to print out for students can be found on the Digital Resource CD (filename: wordlists.pdf).

Teacher Background Information and Tips

Prefixes *dia-* = "through," "across," "thorough" and *per-* = "through," "thorough"

The Greek prefix *dia-,* meaning "through," "across," and "thorough," and the Latin prefix *per-*, meaning "through" and "thorough," appear in important words from math and technology. A *diameter,* for example, is the measurement "through," "across" the center of a circle or other figure; a *diagonal* is a line drawn "through" a polygon connecting nonadjacent angles; a *dialect* is a variety of language spoken "through," "across" a geographical area.

Important math terminology employing Latin *per-* includes *perpendicular* (literally, a vertical line "hanging" "through," "across" a horizontal line) and *percentage* (one hundredth; literally, the number of times a number goes "through" "one hundred"; Latin *cent-* = "100"). The meaning of Latin *per-* as "through" is evident in such academic words as *permeate* (to soak "through"), *perspective* (the point of view acquired by looking "through" a landscape or vista), *perforate* (to poke holes "through"), and *percolate* (to drip "through" small holes or openings).

These prefixes can also have the intensifying meaning of "thorough," as in the word *diagnosis*: a comprehensive and "thorough" understanding of the nature of an illness or problem. The intensifying meaning of *per-* as "thorough" appears in such words as *permanent* (Latin base *man-* = "stay," "remain"; literally, "thoroughly" "lasting"), *perfect* (Latin base *fect-* = "do," "make"; literally, "thoroughly" "done"), *perturbed* (thoroughly disturbed), and *perplexed* (thoroughly confused).

Note: The directional meaning of "through" and the intensifying meaning of "thorough" are connected: when we do something "thoroughly," we often say that we do it "through and through."

For a glossary of words built on these roots, see the Digital Resource CD (filename: rootsglossary.pdf).

Name: _____ Date: _____

About the Root:
Through and Across

Directions: Read the information below. Then answer the questions.

> The Greek prefix *dia-* means "through," "across," and "thorough." The Latin prefix *per-* means "through" and "thorough." Both prefixes appear in important words from math and technology. Greek *dia-* appears in many words that we associate with lines that are drawn "through" or "across" a figure. We can easily visualize many *dia-* words. When we sketch out a figure using simple lines, for example, we create a *diagram* (Greek base *gram-* = "write," "draw"). In geometry, the line we draw "through" the middle of a circle is called the *diameter*. In polygons, a *diagonal* is a line drawn across the figure connecting two noncontiguous angles.
>
> Latin *per* appears in many words and phrases that deal with counting and calculating. When we compute a *percentage*, for example, we count how many times a number can go into one hundred. If we want to compute our *per annum* income, we add up all of our earnings "throughout" an entire year (Latin base *annu-* = "year").

◎ In the two figures below, which line is the *diameter*, and which is the *diagonal*? How do each of these words mean "through" or "across"?

_____

_____

◎ If five people working in an office earn a total of $200 *per* week, what are the *per capita* weekly earnings of the group?

_____

_____

_____

Name: _____ Date: _____

About the Root:
Estimating the Size of an Object

Directions: Read the passage. Then answer the question.

Estimations are guesses. Suppose that you need to estimate the area of an irregularly shaped object. The first thing to do would be to make a diagram of the object. You could measure the perimeter to help you do this. Then, to estimate the area, you can do one of two things.

First, you could try dividing the object up into regular shapes. See how many circles, rectangles, triangles, and so forth you can fit inside the object. Figure out the areas of these shapes, add the areas up, and guess at what's left. You could, for example, guess at the percentage of the remaining area. This is one way to estimate the area of an irregularly shaped object.

Another way is to use a grid. Make a grid of one-inch squares. (You could also make the units on the grid feet or even miles!) Lay the grid over the irregularly shaped object. Now, count the number of full units (square inches, etc.) within the object. Count the units that are half or close to half filled and those that are about a quarter filled. Add all these up to estimate the area of the entire object.

Of course, neither of these methods is perfect. Still, each offers a way to estimate the area of an irregularly shaped object.

◎ Which of the two ways for estimating the area of an irregular object do you prefer? Why?

_____

_____

_____

_____

_____

_____

Name: _____ Date: _____

About the Root:
About the Root:
From Math to Everyday Speech: Diameter

Directions: Read the passage. Then answer the question.

> A *diameter* is a line drawn through the middle of a circle, from one side to the other. The *diameter* bisects the circle into two equal semicircles. The two end points of the *diameter* (see line AB on the diagram) stand at the farthest possible distance from each other. Thus, the *diameter* marks the two points on a circle that are the most distant. It is impossible for any two points on the circle to be farther apart!
>
> *Diametric* is the adjective form of the word *diameter.* We use this word in nonmathematical contexts when we describe positions or views that are far apart. It also describes people who hold opposing views at an extreme level. When we hear debaters say, "My opponent and I are *diametrically opposed* on this issue," we can easily envision a circle with a *diameter* drawn through its middle, with the two points on the circle marking the greatest possible distance. In the same way, two opponents who hold *diametrically opposed* opinions stand "on the opposite sides" of an issue. They could not be farther apart!

◎ Describe two people or groups that are diametrically opposed on an issue. Explain why you think so.

_____

_____

_____

_____

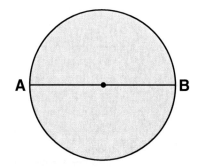

Name: _____ Date: _____

Divide and Conquer:
Words Associated with Through, Across, or Thorough

Directions: Use the Base/Prefix/Suffix Bank to help you identify the roots of the words below. Write the letter from the Definition Bank for the correct word. The *-al* suffix makes one of the words an adjective.

Base/Prefix/Suffix Bank

annu- = "year"   *gon-* = "corner," "angle"   *meter-* = "measure"
cent- = "100"   *gram-* = "write," "draw"

Definition Bank

A. a straight line connecting nonadjacent angles

B. on a yearly basis

C. $\frac{1}{100}$

D. a line drawing

E. the measurement through the middle of a figure, especially a circle

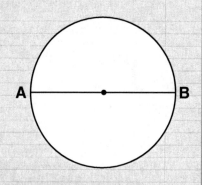

Word	First Base/Prefix Means	Second Base/Suffix Means	Definition
1. diameter			
2. diagonal			
3. percentage			
4. per annum			
5. diagram			

Name: _____ Date: _____

Making Connections:
Unscramble

· ·

Directions: Unscramble the words to fill in the blanks.

1. The two candidates found themselves _____ _____ on domestic issues. (diaacelltmriy deoopps)

2. To compute the circumference of a circle, we use the formula $c = \pi d$. We multiply the length of the _____ by pi. (diaeemrt)

3. As you travel from one region of the country to another, you are likely to hear _____ variations in the language. (diacelt)

4. Before the doctor could prescribe medication, he ran a series of _____ _____ on the patient. (diacginost esstt)

5. The teacher drew a _____ on the board to illustrate the flow of an electrical current. (diaagmr)

6. We need to _____ the problem before we try to fix it. (diaegnos)

7. The students and teachers engaged in a useful _____ over concerns of safety on school property. (diaeglou)

8. In a right triangle, the vertical side is always _____ to the base. (peracdeilnpru)

9. The fraction $\frac{1}{4}$ is equivalent to 25 _____. (percnte)

10. To arrive at the _____ _____ income of the school district, the Census Bureau divided the total income of the district by the number of residences. (per dehhloosu)

11. Use one of the following terms in a sentence: *per diem*, *diagonal*, or *diagnose*.

    _____

    _____

    _____

Prefixes syn-, sym-, syl- and co-, con-, com-

syn-, sym-, syl- and co-, con-, com- = "with," "together," "very"

Standards

Uses a variety of strategies to extend reading vocabulary

Uses common, grade-appropriate Greek or Latin affixes and roots as clues to the meaning of a word

Materials

- *About the Root: Come Together* (page 118)

- *About the Root: What Is a Mathematical Symbol?* (page 119)

- *About the Root: Symmetry* (page 120)

- *Divide and Conquer: Words Associated with Togetherness* (page 121)

- *Making Connections: Fill in the Blank* (page 122)

Teacher Preparation

- Read and review the background information about the prefixes *syn-*, *sym-*, *syl-* and *co-*, *con,- com-* on page 117 to familiarize yourself with words associated with "togetherness."

- Read and review the glossary of the prefixes found on the Digital Resource CD (filename: rootsglossary.pdf) for additional support.

Guided Practice

About the Root

1. Distribute copies of pages 118, 119, and/or 120 to students.

2. Write *syn-*, *sym-*, *syl-* and *co-*, *con-*, *com-* on the board. Tell students these prefixes mean "with," "together," "very."

3. Ask partners to read the passages and answer the questions. You may want to conclude with whole-class discussion.

Divide and Conquer

4. Distribute copies of *Divide and Conquer: Words Associated with Togetherness* (page 121). As you guide students through the activity page, use questions like these to generate discussion about each of the words:

   - Where is the meaning of "with," "together," or "very" in the word _____?

   - Where might you see the word _____?

   - Can you think of an example of _____?

Prefixes syn-, sym-, syl- and co-, con-, com- (cont.)

Making Connections

5. Distribute copies of *Making Connections: Fill in the Blank* (page 122).

6. Ask students to read all of the definitions before completing the activity sheet.

7. You might conclude with a discussion that focuses on root meaning. You might also ask students to define a few of the words in the Word Bank. They could read definitions to classmates, who could guess which words are defined.

Words with syn-, sym-, syl- and co-, con-, com-

asymmetry
asynchronous
co-author
combine
compound
concave
concentric
congruent
contiguous
converge
conversion
convex
coordinates
co-sign
syllable
syllogism
symbiosis
symbol
symmetry
symphony
synchronize
synonym
synthesis
synthesize
synthetic

A list of words to print out for students can be found on the Digital Resource CD (filename: wordlists.pdf).

Teacher Background Information and Tips

Prefixes *syn-, sym-, syl-* and *co-, con-, com-* = "with," "together," "very"

The Greek prefix *syn-, sym-, syl-* and the Latin prefix *co-, con-, com-* mean "with," "together." The Latin prefix can also have the intensifying meaning of "very." These prefixes appear in a large number of everyday vocabulary words and in many specialized words from math, science, and technology.

Words employing Greek bases and prefixes tend to be precise and technical in meaning. This is why they occur so frequently in specialized vocabulary.

The Latin prefix *co-, con-, com-* appears in an extremely large number of everyday and academic vocabulary words. The prefix *co-* is most often attached to intact words. Such words are sometimes written with a hyphen separating *co-* from the original word (e.g., *co-author, co-sign*).

For a glossary of words built on these roots, see the Digital Resource CD (filename: rootsglossary.pdf).

Name: _____ Date: _____

About the Root:
Come Together

· ○ ·

Directions: Read the information. Then answer the questions.

> The Greek prefix *syn-, sym-, syl-* and the Latin prefix *co-, con-, com-* mean "with," "together" and also "very." These prefixes appear in a large number of everyday vocabulary words and in many specialized words from math, science, and technology. Sample words beginning with the Greek prefix include *symmetry, synthetic*, and *symbol.* Sample words beginning with the Latin prefix include *coordinates, concentric, combine*, and *convert*.

◎ The spies said, "Let's synchronize our watches." How does *synchronize* include the idea of "with" or "together"? (**Hint:** *chron-* means "time.")

_____

_____

_____

◎ Look at the concentric circles above. How does *concentric* include the idea of "with" or "together"?

_____

_____

_____

Name: _____ Date: _____

About the Root:
What Is a Mathematical Symbol?

Directions: Read the passage. Then answer the question.

The ancient Greeks relied on *symbols* to identify people and verify messages. When two friends parted ways, they would break a piece of pottery or a small animal bone into two jagged pieces. Each one would keep a part for future reference.

Later, when one friend wished to send a message to the other, he or she would give the messenger his or her broken piece of pottery or bone. When the messenger arrived, the other friend would ask to see the messenger's *symbol* and match it with his or her own. This is what *symbolize* means in Greek: to "put" "together" the two pieces and establish a perfect match.

This is why, even today, we say that a *symbol* is a trustworthy indication of whatever it claims to represent. When we say that the flag is the *symbol* of the country, we mean that we "put together" both flag and country in our minds. The flag makes us think of the country.

Mathematicians use lots of symbols. The Greek letter *pi*, for example is a *symbol* indicating the ratio between the circumference of a circle and its diameter. Do you know any other mathematical symbols? We have symbols for "greater than," "less than," "equal to," "line segment," "angle," "percent," and many more!

◎ Do you think it's a good idea to use symbols in math? Why or why not?

_____

_____

_____

_____

_____

Name: _____ Date: _____

About the Root:
Symmetry

Directions: Read the passage. Then answer the questions.

> *Symmetry* has two related but different definitions. Both relate to the bases on which the word is built. *Sym-* means "with," "together." *Metr-* means "measure." The difference in the definitions has to do with how precise the measurement of similarity is.
>
> Models are sometimes praised for the symmetry of their faces. In this context, symmetry refers to pleasing proportions and a look of balance. Many people equate this sort of imprecise symmetry with beauty.
>
> Symmetry can also be exact. The similarity of symmetrical figures can be proved with formal rules of geometry. You could make two symmetrical pieces of an isosceles triangle by a line from the apex to the midpoint of the base. You could make two symmetrical pieces of a square in two ways. A horizontal line that bisects the vertical sides of a square would yield symmetrical pieces. So would a vertical line that bisects the horizontal sides of the square.

◎ Could you make two symmetrical pieces of a circle? Explain how.

_____

_____

_____

◎ Could you make two symmetrical pieces of a rectangle? Explain how.

_____

_____

_____

Name: _____ Date: _____

Divide and Conquer:
Words Associated with Togetherness

Directions: Use the Base/Prefix/Suffix Bank to help you identify the roots of the words below. Write the letter from the Definition Bank for the correct word. The *-al* suffix makes one of the words an adjective. **Note:** Number 3 contains two prefixes.

Base/Prefix/Suffix Bank

a- = "not," "without"   *metr-* = "measure"   *pound-* = "put," "place"
centr- = "center"   *ordin-* = "order," "arrange"

Definition Bank

A. lack of symmetry or proportion

B. sharing a common center

C. balanced; having corresponding sides or angles of equal measurement

D. assembled from different parts

E. paired numbers which plot a point on a graph

Word	First Base/Prefix Means	Second Base/Suffix Means	Definition
1. symmetrical			
2. coordinates			
3. asymmetry			
4. concentric			
5. compound			

Name: _____ Date: _____

Making Connections:
Fill in the Blank

Directions: Use the words in the Word Bank to complete each sentence.

Word Bank

concentric	syllables	conversion	compound	coordinates
synchronize	combination	converge	contiguous	congruent

Sentences

1. The two angles opposite the equal sides of an isosceles triangle are _____.

2. I tossed a pebble into the pond and watched the waves ripple out in _____ rings.

3. The two sides of an angle are always _____.

4. Let us all _____ our watches before we set out on the field trip.

5. To plot the precise point on a graph, we need to identify both the *x* and the *y* _____.

6. The sudden downturn in the nation's economy is due to a _____ of factors.

7. In the word *multiplication*, I count 5 _____.

8. Parallel lines never _____.

9. The measurement, "2 feet, 5 inches" is a _____ number.

10. According to my _____ table, the decimal 0.75 is equivalent to the fraction $\frac{3}{4}$.

11. Use one of the words *coordinated*, *symbolize*, or *synthetic* in your own sentence:

_____

Prefixes *hypo-* and *sub-*

hypo-, sub- = "below," "under"

Standards

Uses conventions of spelling in written compositions

Determines the meaning of words and phrases as they are used in a text, including figurative, connotative, and technical meanings

Materials

- *About the Root: Below the Surface* (page 126)

- *About the Root: Pythagorean Theorem* (page 127)

- *About the Root: Bell-Shaped Curves and Hypothesis Testing* (page 128)

- *Divide and Conquer: Words Associated with Below or Under* (page 129)

- *Making Connections: Fill in the Blank* (page 130)

Teacher Preparation

- Read and review the background information about the prefixes *hypo-* and *sub-* on page 125 to familiarize yourself with words associated with "below" or "under."

- Read and review the glossary of the prefixes found on the Digital Resource CD (filename: rootsglossary.pdf) for additional support.

Guided Practice

About the Root

1. Distribute copies of pages 126, 127, and/or 128 to students.

2. Write *hypo-* and *sub-* on the board. Tell students these roots mean "below," "under." You may want to ask them to brainstorm words containing the roots.

3. Have pairs of students read the passages and answer the questions. You may want to conclude with whole-class discussion.

Divide and Conquer

4. Distribute copies of *Divide and Conquer: Words Associated with Below or Under* (page 129). As you guide students through the activity page, use questions like these to generate discussion about each of the words:

   - Where is the meaning of "below" or "under" in the word _____?

   - Where might you see the word _____?

   - Can you think of an example of _____?

Prefixes *hypo-* and *sub-* (cont.)

Making Connections

5. Distribute copies of *Making Connections: Fill in the Blank* (page 130).

6. Ask students to skim the page before completing the activity sheet. They can work alone or with partners.

7. You might conclude with a discussion that focuses on root meaning.

Words with *hypo-* and *sub-*

hypocenter
hypodermic
hypodermis
hypoglycemia
hypotension
hypotenuse
hypothermia
hypothesis

subaverage
subdivide
subfloor
submarine
submerge
subnormal
subscribe
subset
substandard
subterranean
subtitles
subtle
subtotal
subtract
subzero

A list of words to print out for students can be found on the Digital Resource CD (filename: wordlists.pdf).

Teacher Background Information and Tips

Prefixes *hypo-* and *sub-* = "below," "under"

Students will already know many words beginning with Latin *sub-*, and they may readily understand the directional meaning of the prefix.

The word *subtraction* is closely associated with the reduction of numbers and the generation of smaller sizes and amounts. This is why the prefix *sub-* is commonly used in math terminology to describe smaller amounts as one "goes down" from larger to ever smaller quantities (e.g., *subset*).

Also in math terminology, words beginning with Latin *sub-* may refer to quantities or measurements that fall "below" a set amount or standard of quality.

Greek-based scientific terminology built on Greek *hypo-* may refer to things that are physically "under," "below" something.

Like Latin *sub-*, Greek *hypo-* is used in words denoting measurements or quantities that fall "below" a standard or a set measurement.

For a glossary of words built on these roots, see the Digital Resource CD (filename: rootsglossary.pdf).

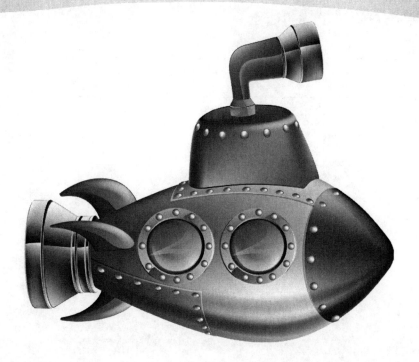

Name: _____ Date: _____

About the Root:
Below the Surface

Directions: Read the information. Then answer the questions.

> The Greek base *hypo-* and the Latin base *sub-* mean "below," "under." *Sub-* appears in a large number of words from general vocabulary and in many words from math. *Hypo-* appears in technical words from science, technology, and math. Words with *sub-* or *hypo-* may describe "below" or "under" physically (e.g., *subfloor*). They may also refer to something that is "below" a standard or norm (e.g., *substandard*).

◎ On a cold day in February, two students failed to wear their coats during recess and suffered a mild case of *hypothermia.* How does the word *hypothermia* include the idea of "below" or "under"? (**Hint:** Greek base *therm-* = "heat," "temperature.")

_____

_____

_____

◎ The teacher said our math quiz scores were *substandard.* How does *substandard* include the idea of "below" or "under"?

_____

_____

_____

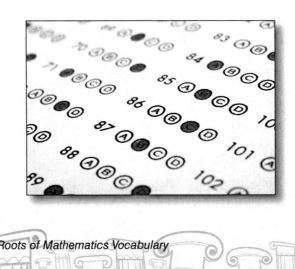

Name: _____   Date: _____

About the Root:
Pythagorean Theorem

Directions: Read the passage. Then answer the question.

You have probably heard of the equation $a^2 + b^2 = c^2$. This is the mathematical expression of the *Pythagorean Theorem*. This theorem defines the relationship among the three sides of a right triangle. This equation holds for any right triangle ABC, where C is the *hypotenuse*. The *hypotenuse* is the slanted side of the triangle across from the right angle. So, if you know the length of two sides of a right triangle, you can figure out the length of the third side.

This theorem was named after the Greek mathematician Pythagoras, who lived around 500 B.C. Many credit him with its discovery. He also developed many proofs about the equation. Some scholars believe that others, such as the ancient Babylonians and the ancient Chinese, also understood the equation.

Pythagoras

The Pythagorean Theorem has many proofs, perhaps the most of any mathematical theorem. Some of these proofs date back thousands of years. Both geometry and algebra have been used to develop proofs. No one knows why mathematicians find this simple equation so fascinating.

◎ *Hypo*- means "under" or "below." *Ten*- means "stretch." How do you think these roots contribute to the meaning of *hypotenuse*?

_____

_____

_____

_____

_____

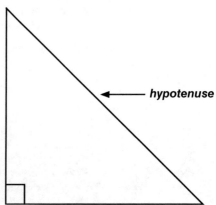

← *hypotenuse*

Right Triangle

Name: _____ Date: _____

About the Root:
Bell-Shaped Curves and Hypothesis Testing

Directions: Read the passage. Then complete the activity.

Probability theory is a branch of mathematics that helps scientists determine the "odds" of something happening. For example, if you flipped a coin 100 times, you'd expect an even split between heads and tails. If the split was 49 – 51 or even 47 – 53, you'd probably think of this as a chance happening. If the split was 25 – 75, though, you would probably suspect a weighted coin.

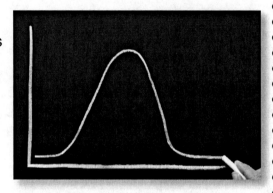

The normal distribution of many variables falls into a "bell-shaped curve." The curve gets its name from its bell shape. The high point of the curve is the average of the variable under study, where most instances fall. To the right and left, the height of the curve falls off, as do instances of the variable under study. Using this curve, mathematicians and statisticians determine the "odds" of something occurring by chance.

Most of these studies involve *hypotheses*. A *hypothesis* is an explanation for something. Scientists make and then test hypotheses. Tests usually involve statistical measurements. These measurements are compared to "normal," using properties of the normal, or bell-shaped, curve. In this way, scientists can determine the "odds" that what they have found could have happened by chance.

◎ Make a hypothesis about grades your class will earn on your next math test. Write it down, and explain how you could test it.

_____

_____

_____

_____

Name: _____ Date: _____

Divide and Conquer:
Words Associated with Below or Under

Directions: Use the Base/Prefix/Suffix Bank to help you identify the roots of the words below. Write the letter from the Definition Bank for the correct word. **Note:** Number 5 contains two prefixes.

Base/Prefix/Suffix Bank

ten- = "stretch," "thin" *tract-* = "pull," "draw," "drag" *thes-* = "put," "place"
divide = di- = "apart" + *therm-* = "warm," "heat,"
  vid- = "separate"   "temperature"

Definition Bank

A. to divide into smaller sections or amounts

B. a theory to be tested

C. low body temperature

D. to reduce; to take one number away from another

E. the side opposite the right angle in a right triangle

Word	First Base/Prefix Means	Second Base/Suffix Means	Definition
1. hypothesis			
2. subtract			
3. hypotenuse			
4. hypothermia			
5. subdivide			

Name: _____ Date: _____

Making Connections:
Fill in the Blank

· ·

Directions: Use the words in the Word Bank to complete each sentence below.

Word Bank

hypodermic	hypotenuse	hypothesis	submultiple	substandard
hypoglycemic	hypothermia	subdivide	subset	subtotal

1. Since 7 x 4 = 28, we know that 7 is a _____ of 28.

2. All elements included within _____ A are also included within the larger Set B.

3. When scientists wish to test a theory, they establish it as a working _____, supposing the theory to be true.

4. After spending six hours in the bitter cold, the children developed _____, which is the precondition for frostbite.

5. The square of the _____ of a right triangle is equal to the sum of the squares of the remaining two sides.

6. The doctor diagnosed the patient as severely _____ because her blood sugar had fallen to severely low levels.

7. After cutting the pizza in half with a pizza cutter, I proceeded to _____ it into twelve pieces so that all my friends could each have at least two slices.

8. This medicine may be taken orally or injected into the body with a _____ needle.

9. After the cashier added up the _____ for all items purchased, he then added sales tax.

10. The testing company determines whether schools have met the standard for scores or have _____ performance.

11. Use the word *substandard*, *hypothetical*, or *subdivision* in a sentence:

_____

_____

Prefixes *hyper-* and *super-*, *sur-*

hyper-, super-, sur- = "over," "above"

Standards

Uses a variety of strategies to extend reading vocabulary

By the end of the year, reads and comprehends literary nonfiction in the grades 6–8 text complexity band proficiently, with scaffolding as needed at the high end of the range

Materials

- *About the Root: Over and Above* (page 134)

- *About the Root: Survey Research* (page 135)

- *About the Root: Another Type of Survey* (page 136)

- *Divide and Conquer: Words Associated with Over or Above* (page 137)

- *Making Connections: Who/What Am I?* (page 138)

Teacher Preparation

- Read and review the background information about the prefixes *hyper-* and *super-*, *sur-* on page 133 to familiarize yourself with words associated with "over" or "above."

- Read and review the glossary of the prefixes found on the Digital Resource CD (filename: rootsglossary.pdf) for additional support.

Guided Practice

About the Root

1. Distribute copies of pages 134, 135, and/or 136 to students.

2. Write *hyper-* and *super-*, *sur-* on the board. Tell students these roots mean "over," "above"; also tell them that these are the opposite of *sub-* and *hypo-*, which they worked with in the last set of lessons.

3. Ask pairs of students to read the passages and answer the questions. You may want to conclude with whole-class sharing or discussion.

Prefixes *hyper-* and *super-*, *sur-* (cont.)

Divide and Conquer

4. Distribute copies of *Divide and Conquer: Words Associated with Over or Above* (page 137). As you guide students through the activity page, use questions like these to generate discussion about each of the words:

- Where is the meaning of "over" or "above" in the word _____?

- Where might you see the word _____?

- Can you think of an example of _____?

Making Connections

5. Distribute copies of *Making Connections: Who/What Am I?* (page 138).

6. Ask students to read all of the definitions before completing the activity sheet.

7. You might conclude with a discussion that focuses on root meaning. You could also ask pairs of students to define some of the words (in their own words); they could read these definitions to others, who could guess at the defined words.

Words with *hyper-* and *super-*, *sur-*

hyperactive	superintendent
hyperbole	superlative
hypercritical	supernumerary
hyperglycemia	supersede
hypersensitive	supersize
hypertension	supersonic
hyperthermia	superstition
hypertrophy	superstructure
hyperventilate	supervise
insuperable	supreme
insurmountable	surcharge
superb	surface
superficial	surfeit
superfluous	surmount
superhighway	surpass
superimpose	survey

A list of words to print out for students can be found on the Digital Resource CD (filename: wordlists.pdf).

Teacher Background Information and Tips

Prefixes *hyper-* and *super-*, *sur-* = "over," "above"

The Greek prefix *hyper-* and the Latin prefix *super-*, *sur-* mean "over," "above." These prefixes appear in a large number of words from academic vocabulary and technical vocabulary. It is useful for students to learn these prefixes within the context of their opposites, the prefixes, *sub-* and *hypo-*, meaning "below," "under" (see previous lesson). Students can benefit from pairing up words with opposite meanings simply by changing the prefix. For example, the opposite of *hypothermia* is *hyperthermia*, the opposite of *substructure* is *superstructure*, and so on.

The prefix *hyper-* is associated with measurement and diagnostic testing that reveals "abnormally high" numbers that fall above a safe range and approach or even enter a danger zone. For this reason, most *hyper-* words describe states that are undesirable; *hyper-* words are more negative than positive in tone. Phrases employing the adverb *overly* often describe words beginning with this prefix. An *overly active* child, for example, is *hyperactive,* and an *overly critical* judge is *hypercritical.*

Words beginning with Latin *super-* often have positive connotations, indicating a "high" quality or a status "over," "above" others (e.g., a *superior* performance, a *superb* meal). Advertisers often use the prefix *super-* to suggest the "high-end" quality of their goods. They may charge a "higher" price for a *super-deluxe* vacation package, or they may give diners the option of *supersizing* a meal. A *superhighway* is designed for "high-speed traffic."

In some words, the prefix *super-*, *sur-* indicates a position that is physically "high" and "above" or "beyond" others. *Lake Superior*, for example, is not only the largest of the Great Lakes (i.e., *superior* in size) but also occupies the northernmost position: on a map, it is "above" the other lakes. Likewise, a land *surveyor* measures a plot of land by looking it "over," either by using a tripod camera or by viewing the site from an airborne location. (On a figurative level, a *survey* is an "overview"; Latin base *vid-*, *vey-* = "see"). Similarly, *survive* means to live beyond or past a time that a person was expected to die.

The word *surface* describes the outer or upper side of an object (Latin base *fac-*, *fici-* = "face"; literally, "above the face"). A *superficial* treatment of a topic deals only with the *surface level* of the issues.

For a glossary of words built on these roots, see the Digital Resource CD (filename: rootsglossary.pdf).

Name: _____   Date: _____

About the Root:
Over and Above
. . . .

Directions: Read the information. Then answer the questions.

> In the last lesson, you learned that *sub-* and *hypo-* mean "below," "under." This lesson focuses on their opposites: The Greek prefix *hyper-* and the Latin prefix *super-*, *sur-* mean "over," "above." These prefixes appear in a large number of words from academic vocabulary and technical vocabulary. Words beginning with Greek *hyper-* often indicate something that surpasses ("goes over and above") a norm or other established measurement or quantity. People suffering from *hyperglycemia*, for example, have "too much" sugar in their blood.

◎ *Hypotension* is low blood pressure. What is *hypertension*? How do you know?

_____

_____

_____

_____

◎ The sound made by a dog whistle is *supersonic.* Do the sound waves produced by this whistle travel above or below the speed of sound that human beings are able to hear? How do you know?

_____

_____

_____

_____

Name: _____   Date: _____

About the Root:
Survey Research

. . . .

Directions: Read the passage. Then answer the question.

> Social scientists sometimes use survey research to get an overview of how people feel about issues. Businesses sometimes use surveys to see what people think about their products or services. Even websites sometimes use surveys.
>
> People may be surveyed in person, over the telephone, in the mail, or online. Three types of questions may be used:
>
> ◎ Open-ended questions simply ask people what they think. For example, a hotel survey might ask people to "describe your recent stay with us in your own words."
>
> ◎ Two types of close-ended questions may also be used. One type of close-ended question offers choices for response. Again, using the hotel survey as an example, a survey might ask, "Which of these was most important in your decision to stay with us? A) price, B) location, C) reputation for service, D) loyalty program."
>
> ◎ The other type of close-ended question consists of statements followed by response options. A hotel survey might ask people to respond to statements like "Having a hotel close to the center of a city is important to me" or "I really don't need fancy services like spas in hotels." People then respond on a scale of 1–5 saying how much they agree (1) or disagree (5) with the statements.
>
> Some surveys include demographic items like age or gender. This is so that differences in results among subgroups can be understood.

◎ Which of the question types do you think is strongest? Why?

_____

_____

_____

Name: _____ Date: _____

About the Root:

Another Type of Survey

Directions: Read the passage. Then answer the question.

Perhaps you have seen "Surveying Ahead" road signs on the highway. Up the road a little, you find a person or two peering through instruments. What are these people doing? And how do they use math?

Surveying is an outdoor activity that involves measurement in which surveyors look over or examine portions of land. This can be done on a small scale, such as measuring for the location of a building. It can also be done on a very large scale, such as determining the path of a proposed highway or the boundaries between communities or even countries.

Surveyors' work is something like that of seafaring navigators, who gathered measurement information from the stars to chart their way. Surveyors use telescopes instead of stars to find points they can measure. If you think about the challenges in this type of measurement, you can probably see that math is involved. In fact, surveyors use both plane geometry and trigonometry every day.

Surveyors show their results in maps, which are two-dimensional representations of part of Earth's surface.

◎ Explain how surveyors might need to use geometry.

_____

_____

_____

_____

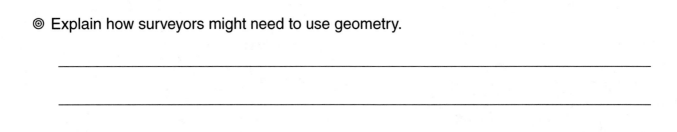

Name: _____ Date: _____

Divide and Conquer:
Words Associated with Over or Above

Directions: Use the Base/Prefix/Suffix Bank to help you identify the roots of the words below. Write the letter from the Definition Bank for the correct word. **Note:** Number 3 contains two prefixes.

Base/Prefix/Suffix Bank

charge = "charge"	*pos-* = "put," "place"	*tens-* = "stretch," "thin"
im- = "in," "on"	*son-* = "sound"	*ventil-* = "wind," "air"

Definition Bank

A. to ingest too much air

B. faster than the frequency of audible sound

C. high blood pressure

D. an additional fee or amount

E. to place one thing or figure on top of another

Word	First Base/Prefix Means	Second Base/Suffix Means	Definition
1. surcharge			
2. supersonic			
3. superimpose			
4. hypertension			
5. hyperventilate			

Name: _____ Date: _____

Making Connections:
Who/What Am I?

Directions: Match each word or phrase in the first column with its speaker in the second column.

Word/Phrase	Speaker
_____ 1. hyperactive	A. I cannot be beaten.
_____ 2. surcharge	B. I am excessive and leftover.
_____ 3. supernumerary	C. I am better than the rest.
_____ 4. superfluous	D. I am eerie, unexplainable by the laws of nature.
_____ 5. hypertrophy	E. I am an overgrown muscle.
_____ 6. superior	F. I am added on top of other fees and costs.
_____ 7. supernatural	G. I cannot sit still.
_____ 8. insuperable	H. I am a walk-on in a mob scene for the school play.
_____ 9. Supreme Court	I. We are the highest court in the land.
_____ 10. hypercritical	J. I find fault with everything, down to the last detail.

11. Use the word *hypercritical*, *supersensitive*, or *surmount* in a sentence:

_____

_____

_____

Base *meter-, metr-*

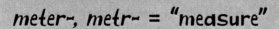

meter-, metr- = "measure"

Standards

Uses conventions of spelling in written compositions

Uses common, grade-appropriate Greek or Latin affixes and roots as clues to the meaning of a word

Materials

- *About the Root: Measure Up* (page 142)

- *About the Root: How Did Geometry Get Its Name?* (page 143)

- *About the Root: Counting Steps* (page 144)

- *Divide and Conquer: Words Associated with Measuring* (page 145)

- *Making Connections: I Count!* (page 146)

Teacher Preparation

- Read and review the background information about the base *meter-, metr-* on page 141 to familiarize yourself with words associated with "measuring."

- Read and review the glossary of the base found on the Digital Resource CD (filename: rootsglossary.pdf) for additional support.

Guided Practice

About the Root

1. Distribute copies of pages 142, 143, and/or 144 to students.

2. Write *meter-, metr-* on the board. Tell students that this base means "measure."

3. Ask individuals to read the passages and respond to the questions. After a few minutes, invite sharing.

4. Conclude with whole-class discussion.

Divide and Conquer

5. Distribute copies of *Divide and Conquer: Words Associated with Measuring* (page 145). As you guide students through the activity page, use questions like these to generate discussion about each of the words:

- Where is the meaning of "measure" in the word _____?

- Where might you see the word _____?

- Can you think of an example of _____?

Base meter-, metr- (cont.)

Making Connections

6. Distribute copies of *Making Connections: I Count!* (page 146).

7. Ask students to read all of the definitions before completing the activity sheet.

8. To conclude, you might ask pairs of students to define some of the words. They can then read the definitions to others, who can guess the words being defined.

Words with meter-, metr-

- barometer
- centimeter
- chronometer
- decameter
- decimeter
- diameter
- geometry
- hectometer
- kilometer
- meter
- metrology
- metronome
- millimeter
- odometer
- pedometer
- perimeter
- photometer
- speedometer
- symmetry
- thermometer
- trigonometry

A list of words to print out for students can be found on the Digital Resource CD (filename: wordlists.pdf).

Teacher Background Information and Tips

Base *meter-, metr-* = "measure"

The Greek base *meter-, metr-*, meaning "measure," appears in many words from science, math, and technology. Scientific implements of precise measurement are often given a name ending in the Greek base *meter*. For example, a *thermometer* measures temperature (Greek base *thermo-* = "heat"), an *odometer* measures distance traveled by a vehicle (Greek base *od(o)-* = "way"), and a *barometer* measures atmospheric pressure (Greek base *bar(o)-* = "weight," "heavy").

The base *meter-, metr-* also provides the cornerstone of measurement terminology within the *metric system* (e.g., *meter, decimeter, decameter*). These words refer to the official units of "measurement" as determined by the SI (International System of Units). See below for a brief explanation of the origin of the *metric system*.

The Origin of the Metric System

The metric system is officially known as the International System of Units, abbreviated as SI. The system was developed in France in 1790, when the National Assembly of France asked the French Academy of Sciences to develop a universal standard for all weights and measures. The establishment of such a system, it was believed, would greatly help scientists and technicians throughout the world to share their research and findings with one another. A universal system of weights and measures would greatly facilitate trade and commerce among nations.

In keeping with the worldwide scope of this system, the unit of measurement was to be based on a fraction of Earth's circumference. At that time, scientists largely believed that the circumference of Earth was a perfect circle. Using a decimal system (i.e., a base of 10), the French Academy designated the universal unit of distance as one ten millionth of the distance from the equator to the North Pole, along a vertical line running through Paris. In keeping with the scientific tradition of using Greek bases for scientific terminology, the French Academy originally called this unit a "meter," (which they spelled as "metre"), from the Greek word *metron* meaning "measure."

Subsequent attempts to refine and perfect the calculation of the meter have been based on other criteria besides the Earth's circumference, which we now know is not a perfect circle. These modifications have included the development of the Prototype Meter Bar, which is an alloy of platinum and iridium etched with marks as well as measurements based on wavelengths of light. Attempts to develop increasingly precise measurement of the meter have given rise to a new word: *metrology*, which means "study of the meter."

For a glossary of words built on these roots, see the Digital Resource CD (filename: rootsglossary.pdf).

Name: _____ Date: _____

About the Root:
Measure Up

. . . .

Directions: Read the information. Then answer the questions.

The Greek base *meter-, metr-* means "measure." This base appears in many words from science, math, and technology, especially at the ends of words. Of course, *meter* is also a word all by itself. Since human beings are interested in quantification and measuring everything they can, scientists have come up with many devices to measure many different things. Many of these devices have become household words. For example, our cars are equipped with *speedometers* to measure our speed and with *odometers* to measure the distance or mileage traveled. We have *barometers* to measure air pressure and *anemometers* to measure wind speed. People who walk for exercise like to wear *pedometers* to measure the distance they travel on foot!

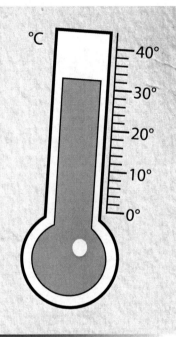

◎ What does a *thermometer* measure? (**Hint:** Greek base *thermo-* = "heat," "warm," "temperature")

_____

_____

◎ What is a *diameter*? (**Hint:** Greek prefix *dia-* = "through," "across")

_____

Name: _____ Date: _____

About the Root:

How Did Geometry Get Its Name?

Directions: Read the passage. Then answer the question.

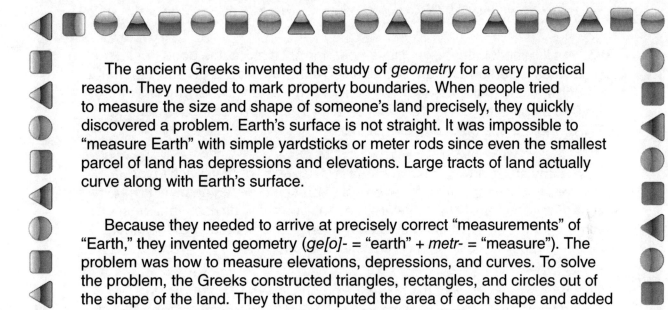

The ancient Greeks invented the study of *geometry* for a very practical reason. They needed to mark property boundaries. When people tried to measure the size and shape of someone's land precisely, they quickly discovered a problem. Earth's surface is not straight. It was impossible to "measure Earth" with simple yardsticks or meter rods since even the smallest parcel of land has depressions and elevations. Large tracts of land actually curve along with Earth's surface.

Because they needed to arrive at precisely correct "measurements" of "Earth," they invented geometry (*ge[o]-* = "earth" + *metr-* = "measure"). The problem was how to measure elevations, depressions, and curves. To solve the problem, the Greeks constructed triangles, rectangles, and circles out of the shape of the land. They then computed the area of each shape and added them together to arrive at the total measurement. And geometry was born!

◎ On a sheet of paper, draw an irregular shape that might be a tract of land. Now try to fill it completely with rectangles, triangles, and circles. Write a sentence or two about how well this worked.

_____

_____

_____

_____

_____

Name: _____   Date: _____

About the Root:
Counting Steps

Directions: Read the passage. Then answer the questions on a separate sheet of paper.

We've all been told that exercise is good for us. It promotes good health and even elevates a person's mood. We also know that walking is great exercise. But how much walking makes sense? Exercise scientists say those who walk fewer than 5,000 steps each day have a "sedentary" lifestyle, while those who take 10,000 or more steps each day are "active."

How many steps do you take each day? Are you sedentary, active, or somewhere in between? With a *pedometer*, you could get an answer. (The Greek base *ped-* means "foot.") Pedometers are small portable devices that detect hip motion and, thus, count steps. Because the lengths of people's strides differ, pedometers must be calibrated before their first use.

Thousands of years ago, the ancient Romans invented an *odometer* calibrated for steps to measure distance. (The Greek base *odo-* means "way.") Thomas Jefferson, who introduced pedometers in the United States, wrote about ancient odometers.

Of course, today's pedometers are more technologically advanced than they were in Jefferson's time. A metal ball sliding back and forth, or a pendulum, once triggered the step count. Today, sophisticated software serves this purpose.

Pedometers were once used mostly for sports training or physical fitness. Now they're more popular because of the link between physical activity and overall health. So get walking!

◎ How could you estimate the number of steps you take each day without using a pedometer?

◎ Divide and conquer *pedometer* and *odometer*. Tell what each word means. Also tell how they are alike and different.

Name: _____   Date: _____

Divide and Conquer:
Words Associated with Measuring

Directions: Use the Base/Prefix/Suffix Bank to help you identify the roots of the words below. Write the letter from the Definition Bank for the correct word.

Base/Prefix/Suffix Bank

dia- = "across," "through"   *peri-* = "around"   *bar(o)-* = "weight," "pressure"
od(o)- = "road," "distance"   *sym-* = "with," "together"

Definition Bank

A. balance; equal measurement of corresponding sides

B. a device that measures atmospheric (air) pressure

C. the measure through the middle of a circle

D. the distance around a polygon

E. a device that measures distance traveled by a vehicle

Word	First Base/Prefix Means	Second Base/Suffix Means	Definition
1. perimeter			
2. barometer			
3. symmetry			
4. odometer			
5. diameter			

Name: _____ Date: _____

Making Connections:
I Count!

. . . .

Directions: Match each numerical term or measurement device in the first column with its speaker in the second column.

Measurement Device/
Numerical Term   **Speaker**

_____ **1.** speedometer   **A.** I measure the distance walked by foot.

_____ **2.** kilometer   **B.** I measure about 39.37 inches.

_____ **3.** perimeter   **C.** I am the sum total of the 4 sides of a quadrangle.

_____ **4.** pedometer   **D.** I am a length of 1,000 meters.

_____ **5.** thermometer   **E.** I am $\frac{1}{1,000}$ of a meter.

_____ **6.** meter   **F.** I measure how fast your car is travelling.

_____ **7.** metronome   **G.** I am an extremely precise time-measuring device.

_____ **8.** millimeter   **H.** I measure time while music is being played.

_____ **9.** odometer   **I.** I measure temperature.

_____ **10.** chronometer   **J.** I measure the miles or kilometers traveled by a car.

11. What do you think a *photometer* measures? How can you tell?

_____

_____

_____

Numerical Bases dec(i)-, cent(i)-, and mill(i)-

$$dec(i)\text{-} = \text{“}\frac{1}{10}\text{”}$$

$$cent(i)\text{-} = \text{“}\frac{1}{100}\text{”}$$

$$mill(i)\text{-} = \text{“}\frac{1}{1{,}000}\text{”}$$

Standards

Uses a variety of strategies to extend reading vocabulary

Determines the meaning of words and phrases as they are used in a text, including figurative, connotative, and technical meanings

Materials

- *About the Root: Latin Metric Terminology* (page 150)

- *About the Root: Metric System—The Basics* (page 151)

- *About the Root: December* (page 152)

- *Divide and Conquer: Latin Words Associated with Ten, Hundred, and Thousand* (page 153)

- *Making Connections: Equivalents* (page 154)

Teacher Preparation

- Read and review the background information about the numerical bases *dec(i)-, cent(i)-,* and *mill(i)-* on page 149 to familiarize yourself with words associated with "ten," "hundred," and "thousand."

- Read and review the glossary of the numerical bases found on the Digital Resource CD (filename: rootsglossary.pdf) for additional support.

Guided Practice

About the Root

1. Distribute copies of pages 150, 151, and/or 152 to students.

2. Tell students that the next few lessons will focus on small metric measures: $dec(i)\text{-} = \text{“}\frac{1}{10}\text{,”}$ $cent(i)\text{-} = \text{“}\frac{1}{100}\text{,”}$ and $mill(i)\text{-} = \text{“}\frac{1}{1{,}000}\text{.”}$

3. Ask pairs of students to read the passages and answer the questions.

4. Conclude with whole-class discussion.

Divide and Conquer

5. Distribute copies of *Divide and Conquer: Latin Words Associated with Ten, Hundred, and Thousand* (page 153). As you guide students through the activity page, use questions like these to generate discussion about each of the words:

- Where is the meaning of "$\frac{1}{10}$," "$\frac{1}{100}$," or "$\frac{1}{1{,}000}$" in the word _____?

- Where might you see the word _____?

- Can you think of an example of _____?

Numerical Bases dec(i)-, cent(i)-, and mill(i)- (cont.)

Making Connections

6. Distribute copies of *Making Connections: Equivalents* (page 154).

7. Ask students to skim the page before completing the activity sheet.

8. Conclude by asking partners to write out reasons for a few of their answers; then share these.

Metric system terms with dec(i)-, cent(i)-, mill(i)-

cent

centigrade

centigram

centimeter

decigram

decimal

decimeter

micromillimeter

mill

milligram

milliliter

millimeter

percent

A list of words to print out for students can be found on the Digital Resource CD (filename: wordlists.pdf).

Teacher Background Information and Tips

Numerical Bases $dec(i)\text{-} = \text{"}\frac{1}{10}\text{"}$, $cent(i)\text{-} = \text{"}\frac{1}{100}\text{"}$, and $mill(i)\text{-} = \text{"}\frac{1}{1,000}\text{"}$

In Unit I, students learned that the Latin numerical bases *cent-* and *mill-* mean, respectively, "100" and "1,000." Thus, a *century* consists of 100 years, and a *centennial* celebrates a 100-year anniversary. Likewise, there are 1,000 years in a *millennium*, and a *millionaire* owns 1,000 units of 1,000 dollars.

When applied to the metric system, however, these Latin bases indicate fractions, not multiples, of measurement. Greek numerical bases, by contrast, (presented in the next lesson) are used to indicate multiples of measurement. The International System of Units (SI) deliberately employed Greek and Latin numerical bases with this distinction.

Thus, in metric terminology, *cent(i)-* refers to $\frac{1}{100}$ of a unit of measurement, and *mill(i)-* refers to $\frac{1}{1,000}$ of a unit of measurement. A *centimeter*, for example, is $\frac{1}{100}$ of a meter; a *millimeter* is $\frac{1}{1,000}$ of a meter. The Latin numerical base *dec(i)-* means $\frac{1}{10}$. A *decimal* point, for example, indicates $\frac{1}{10}$.

Since the metric system is based on 10, converting units of measurement is easy for students. Keeping the numerical meaning of Latin *dec(i)-*, *cent(i)-*, and *mill(i)-* in mind, students can convert each metric term into a fraction of $\frac{1}{10}$, $\frac{1}{100}$, or $\frac{1}{1,000}$. After converting "number words" into their corresponding fractions, students then apply the basic rules of fraction simplification.

Students can also use base 10 to convert fractions and percentages into decimals. For example, because *percent* means "through 100," we convert decimals into percentages by moving the decimal point two places to the right: 0.75 = 75 percent.

◎ 10 decimeters = 1 meter ($\frac{10}{10} = 1$)

◎ 100 centimeters = 1 meter ($\frac{100}{100} = 1$)

◎ 10 centimeters = 1 decimeter ($\frac{10}{100} = \frac{1}{10}$)

◎ 10 millimeters = 1 centimeter ($\frac{10}{1,000} = \frac{1}{100}$)

◎ 1,000 millimeters = 1 meter ($\frac{1,000}{1,000} = 1$)

Name: _____   Date: _____

About the Root:
Latin Metric Terminology

Directions: Read the information. Then complete the sentences below.

> In Unit I of this book, we learned that the Latin numerical bases *cent-* and *mill-* mean, respectively, "100" and "1,000." A *century* is 100 years, for example, and a *millennium* is 1,000 years.
>
> In the metric system, these bases indicate fractions of measurement. In metric terminology, *cent(i)-* refers to $\frac{1}{100}$ of a unit of measurement and *mill(i)-* refers to $\frac{1}{1,000}$ of a unit of measurement. A *centimeter*, for example, is $\frac{1}{100}$ of a meter. Similarly, a *millimeter* is $\frac{1}{1,000}$ of a meter. The Latin numerical base *dec(i)-* means $\frac{1}{10}$. A *decimal* point, for example, indicates $\frac{1}{10}$.

◎ A centimeter is _____ of a meter. There are _____ centimeters in a meter.

◎ A millimeter is _____ of a meter. There are _____ millimeters in a meter.

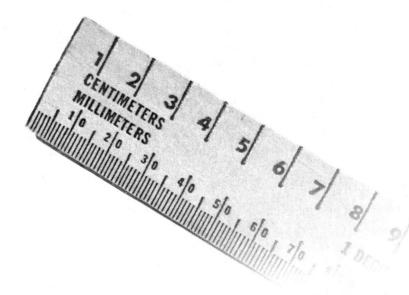

Name: _____   Date: _____

About the Root:
Metric System—The Basics

Directions: Read the passage. Then answer the question.

The metric system is easy to learn and use. The system has several basic units. Units are changed using multiples of 10. The basic units of measurement are the *gram* for weight, the *liter* for volume (especially of liquids), and the *meter* for length. A gram is about the weight of a kidney bean. A liter is a bit more than a quart. These units are exactly the same all around the world.

If you need bigger or smaller amounts, prefixes come in handy. The prefix *kilo-* means 1,000 times bigger. A liter of water weighs a *kilogram*, which is 1,000 grams. The prefix *deci-* means 10 times smaller. *Centi-* means 100 times smaller, and *milli-* means 1,000 times smaller. A *centimeter* is about the width of your little fingernail. A *millimeter* is about the width of a piece of uncooked angel hair pasta. A *milliliter* weighs about a gram.

◎ Do you think it's a good idea for all people everywhere to use the same system for measuring? Why?

_____

_____

_____

_____

_____

_____

Name: _____ Date: _____

About the Root:
December

. . . .

Directions: Read the passage. Then answer the question.

> We all know that December is the 12th month in the calendar. But the Latin base *dec(i)-* means "tenth." A root meaning "tenth" in the twelfth month? Why is this so?
>
> **March 2013**
> | SUNDAY | MONDAY | TUESDAY | WEDNESDAY | THURSDAY | FRIDAY | SATURDAY |
> |---|---|---|---|---|---|---|
> | | | | | | 1 | 2 |
> | 3 | 4 | 5 | 6 | 7 | 8 | 9 |
> | 10 | 11 | 12 | 13 | 14 | 15 | 16 |
> | 17 | 18 | 19 | 20 | 21 | 22 | 23 |
> | 24 | 25 | 26 | 27 | 28 | 29 | 30 |
> | 31 | | | | | | |
>
> The ancient Romans began their calendar year in the month of March. The Romans believed that they were descendants of the god Mars, so they began their calendar year with the month named in his honor: March.
>
> If we count the months of the year by using March as the starting point, we find an interesting pattern: April, May, June, July, and August follow as the 2nd, 3rd, 4th, 5th, and 6th months, respectively. Then come September (the 7th month; the root *sept[i]-* means "seven"), October (the 8th month; the root *oct[a/o]-* means "eight"), November (the 9th month; the root *nov[em]-* means "nine"), and December (the 10th month).
>
> In modern times, of course, we start our calendar with the month of January. But we have kept the original Latin names. As a result, the months September, October, November, and December are now, respectively, the 9th, 10th, 11th, and 12th months of the year.

◎ Do you think it matters if the year is 10 months or 12 months? Why?

_____

_____

_____

_____

_____

Name: _____   Date: _____

Divide and Conquer:
Latin Words Associated with Ten, Hundred, and Thousand

Directions: The words in the list below employ roots that you have already learned in this book. See how good your memory is by identifying the roots. *X* means the word does not contain that element. Write the letter from the Definition Bank for the correct word.

Definition Bank

A. $\frac{1}{10}$ of a meter

B. a fraction indicating $\frac{1}{10}$

C. $\frac{1}{100}$ of a dollar

D. $\frac{1}{1,000}$ of a meter

E. $\frac{1}{100}$ of a meter

Word	First Base/Prefix Means	Second Base/Suffix Means	Definition
1. decimeter			
2. cent		X	
3. decimal		X	
4. millimeter			
5. centimeter			

Name: _____   Date: _____

Making Connections:
Equivalents

. . . .

Directions: Match each numerical term or number in the first column with its equivalent in the second column.

Numerical Term/Number	**Equivalent**
_____ 1. 0.5	**A.** 0.25 (25 percent)
_____ 2. $\frac{1}{4}$	**B.** 2 meters
_____ 3. 100 centimeters	**C.** 3.5 meters
_____ 4. 100 millimeters	**D.** 1 decimeter
_____ 5. 100 cents	**E.** $\frac{1}{1,000}$ of a second
_____ 6. 20 decimeters	**F.** $\frac{1}{2}$
_____ 7. 10 millimeters	**G.** 1 meter
_____ 8. millisecond	**H.** 1 centimeter
_____ 9. 350 centimeters	**I.** 3,000 millimeters
_____ 10. 3 meters	**J.** 1 dollar

11. Is a *centimeter* longer or shorter than a *millimeter*? How can you tell?

_____

_____

A mill is $\frac{1}{1,000}$ of a cent. Although we have no coin smaller than a cent, we sometimes find this term on tax proposals and voting ballots. Communities often raise public funds by charging taxes set at a certain number of mills. These are called *mill levies*.

Numerical Bases deca-, hect(o)-, and kil(o)-

deca- = "10"

hect(o)- = "100"

kil(o)- = "1,000"

Standards

Uses conventions of spelling in written compositions

By the end of the year, reads and comprehends literary nonfiction in the grades 6–8 text complexity band proficiently, with scaffolding as needed at the high end of the range

Materials

- *About the Root: Greek Metric Terminology* (page 158)

- *About the Root: Decathlons* (page 159)

- *About the Root: Megabytes and Gigabytes* (page 160)

- *Divide and Conquer: Greek Words Associated with Ten, Hundred, and Thousand* (page 161)

- *Making Connections: Magic Square* (page 162)

Teacher Preparation

- Read and review the background information about the numerical bases *deca-, hect(o)-,* and *kil(o)-* on page 157 to familiarize yourself with words associated with "ten," "hundred," and "thousand."

- Read and review the glossary of the numerical bases found on the Digital Resource CD (filename: rootsglossary.pdf) for additional support.

Guided Practice

About the Root

1. Distribute copies of pages 158, 159, and/or 160 to students.

2. Tell students that the next few lessons focus on prefixes for large metric measures: *deca-* (10), *hect(o)-* (100), and *kil(o)-* (1,000). You may want to write these on the board.

3. Ask individuals to read the passages and answer the questions. After a few minutes, invite sharing.

4. Conclude with whole-class discussion.

Divide and Conquer

5. Distribute copies of *Divide and Conquer: Greek Words Associated with Ten, Hundred, and Thousand* (page 161). As you guide students through the activity page, use questions like these to generate discussion about each of the words:

- Where is the meaning of "10," "100," or "1,000" in the word _____?

- Where might you see the word _____?

Numerical Bases deca-, hect(o)- and kil(o)- (cont.)

- Can you think of an example of _____?

Making Connections

6. Distribute copies of *Making Connections: Magic Square* (page 162).

7. Students can complete the Magic Square independently or with partners. Invite discussion of answers to the last question.

Metric system terms with deca-, hect(o)-, kil(o)-

decade
decagram
decaliter
decameter
hectometer
kilobyte
kilogram
kiloliter
kilometer

A list of words to print out for students can be found on the Digital Resource CD (filename: wordlists.pdf).

Teacher Background Information and Tips

Numerical Bases *deca-* = "10", *hect(o)-* = "100", and *kil(o)-* = "1,000"

The terminology of the metric system employs Greek numerical bases for large units of measurement: *deca-* means "10," *hect(o)-* means "100," and *kil(o)-* means "1,000." Students may be familiar with some of these bases from such words as *decade* (a period of 10 years), *decathlon* (a 10-sport event), *kilometer* (a distance of 1,000 meters), and *kilogram* (a weight of 1,000 grams, often abbreviated as "*kilo*").

All three of these Greek bases are pronounced with a hard *c* (/k/ sound): *deca*, *hect(o)-*, and *kil(o)-*. For this reason, some mathematicians opt to spell *deca-* as *deka-*. Either spelling is acceptable both when the words are written in full (e.g., *decameter-dekameter, decagram-dekagram, decaliter-dekaliter*) and when abbreviated (e.g., *dam-dkm, dag-dkg, dal-dkl*). Latin bases *dec(i)-* and *cent(i)-*, on the other hand, are pronounced with the soft *c* (/s/) .

Converting *deca-, hect(o)-,* and *kil(o)-* to other units of measurement within the metric system is based on multiples of 10.

* 10 meters = 1 decameter (10 x 1 = 10)

* 10 decameters = 1 hectometer (10 x 10 = 100)

* 10 hectometers = 1 kilometer (10 x 100 = 1,000)

Name: _____   Date: _____

About the Root:
Greek Metric Terminology

Directions: Read the information. Then answer the questions.

> This lesson focuses on three Greek bases that describe large units of measurement. *Deca-* means 10, *hect(o)-* means 100, and *kil(o)-* means 1,000. All three of these bases are pronounced with a /k/ sound. (Latin bases *dec[i]-* and *cent[i]-*, on the other hand, are pronounced with the soft /c/—like an /s/.) Here is a helpful hint for remembering that these Greek roots are pronounced with the hard /c/ sound: "It's Greek to me!" In the word Greek, the hard *g* and *k* sounds resemble the hard *c* sounds in *deca-*, *hect(o)-*, and *kil(o)-*.

◎ How many years are in a *decade*?

_____

◎ How many meters are in a *kilometer*?

_____

◎ What is longer, a *millimeter* or a *kilometer*? How do you know?

_____

_____

_____

Name: _____ Date: _____

About the Root:
Decathlons

. . . .

Directions: Read the passage. Then answer the question.

Decathlons are track-and-field events. They are held at each summer Olympics and also at other times. Knowing the meaning of *deca-*, can you guess how many events they include? That's right—ten. These are the events: races of three different lengths, hurdles, high and long jumps, discus, javelin, shot put, and pole vault. Usually, decathlons are held over two days. Each event is scored. The athlete who amasses the best combined score is declared the winner.

The American Olympian, Jim Thorpe, competed in the decathlon in the Stockholm Olympics in 1912. King Gustav V of Sweden was so impressed with Thorpe's performance that he said, "You, sir, are the world's greatest athlete." This label stuck. Even today the Olympic decathlon winner is called "the world's greatest athlete."

32 USA

Jim Thorpe, Star at Stockholm

Why do you think decathlon winners are considered such great athletes?

_____

_____

_____

_____

_____

_____

Name: _____ Date: _____

About the Root:
Megabytes and Gigabytes

Directions: Read the passage. Then answer the questions.

Computers operate on a binary system. 0s and 1s are used for all data. The smallest unit of data in a computer is called a *bit*. This is an abbreviation of *binary digit*. A *byte* is an 8-bit-long data string. That's not much data, though. As computers develop, we need words to describe larger amounts of data storage space and disk space.

Prefixes to the rescue! The prefix *kilo-* means 1,000. The prefixes *mega-* and *giga-* refer to powers of 1,000. Thus, 1 *kilobyte* (KB) = 1,000 bytes, 1 *megabyte* (MB) = 1,000,000 bytes or 1,000 KBs, and 1 *gigabyte* (GB) = 1,000,000,000 bytes or 1,000 MBs.

When describing computer memory, *kilobyte, megabyte,* and *gigabyte* are based on 1,024 instead of 1,000. No one is sure why this happened. Scientists think it was the result of common practice in the early days of computing.

As computers continue to become more powerful, we need more prefixes to describe the sizes of data storage and disk space. Next in line after gigabyte is *terabyte* (TB), which is one trillion bytes, or 1,000 gigabytes. These are interesting words: The Greek base *giga-* means "giant," as in the adjective *gigantic*. The Greek base *tera-* means "monster." So, a gigabyte is gigantic, but a terabyte is monstrously large! Here's a way to think about these extra large sizes: 1 TB could hold 1,000 copies of an encyclopedia, and 10 TBs could hold all the printed material in the Library of Congress!

◎ Does the difference in powers of 1,000 or powers of 1,024 make much difference for an ordinary computer user? Why?

_____

_____

◎ Why do contemporary computers require more data storage space than computers in previous years?

_____

_____

Name: _____ Date: _____

Divide and Conquer:
Greek Words Associated with Ten, Hundred, and Thousand

Directions: Use the Base/Prefix/Suffix Bank to help you identify the roots of the words below. Write the letter from the Definition Bank for the correct word.

> **Base/Prefix/Suffix Bank**
>
> *athl-* = "contest," "struggle"   *liter-* = "liter," "liquid measurement"

Definition Bank

A. a sporting contest in 10 events

B. a distance of 1,000 meters

C. a distance of 100 meters

D. a period of 10 years

E. a liquid measurement of 1,000 liters

Word	First Base/Prefix Means	Second Base/Suffix Means	Definition
1. kiloliter			
2. hectometer			
3. decathlon			
4. kilometer			
5. decade			

Name: _____   Date: _____

Making Connections:
Magic Square

Directions: Match each numerical term or number in the first column with its equivalent in the second column. Then put the number of the answer in the magic square. You can check your answers when you finish. All the rows and all the columns will add up to the same number. You will not use all of the terms.

Numerical Term/Number

_____ **A.** 10 centimeters

_____ **B.** 200 decameters

_____ **C.** 350 meters

_____ **D.** 10 decades

_____ **E.** 35 hectometers

_____ **F.** 1,000 meters

_____ **G.** 10 decameters

_____ **H.** 1 kilowatt

_____ **I.** 500 meters

_____ **J.** 500 decameters

Equivalent

1. 5 kilometers

2. 2 kilometers

3. 5 kilometers

4. 1 century

5. 1 hectometer

6. 3.5 kilometers

7. 3.5 hectometers

8. 1 kilometer

9. 1 decimeter

10. 1,000 watts

A:	B:	C:
D:	E:	F:
G:	H:	I:

Magic Number:

_____

Is a *kilometer* longer or shorter than a *hectometer*? How can you tell?

_____

_____

Base *graph-, gram-*

graph-, gram- = "write," "draw"

Standards

Uses a variety of strategies to extend reading vocabulary

Uses common, grade-appropriate Greek or Latin affixes and roots as clues to the meaning of a word

Materials

- *About the Root: Write About It* (page 166)
- *About the Root: Pictograms* (page 167)
- *About the Root: Measuring Solids* (page 168)
- *Divide and Conquer: Words Associated with Writing* (page 169)
- *Making Connections: Equivalents* (page 170)

Teacher Preparation

- Read and review the background information about the base *graph-, gram-* on page 165 to familiarize yourself with words associated with "writing" or "drawing."

- Read and review the glossary of the base found on the Digital Resource CD (filename: rootsglossary.pdf) for additional support.

Guided Practice

About the Root

1. Distribute copies of pages 166, 167, and/or 168 to students.

2. Write *graph-, gram-* on the board. Tell students that these mean "write" or "draw." You might also point out that *gram* and *graph* are words in their own rights.

3. Ask pairs of students to read and discuss the passages and answer the questions.

4. Conclude with whole-class discussion.

Divide and Conquer

5. Distribute copies of *Divide and Conquer: Words Associated with Writing* (page 169). As you guide students through the activity page, use questions like these to generate discussion about each of the words:

   - Where is the meaning of "write" or "draw" in the word _____?
   - Where might you see the word _____?
   - Can you think of an example of _____?

Base graph-, gram- (cont.)

Making Connections

6. Distribute copies of *Making Connections: Equivalents* (page 170).

7. Ask students to skim the activity page before completing it.

8. To conclude this activity, you might ask pairs of students to write out math problems that prove a few of their responses.

Words with graph-, gram-

autobiography
biography
cartography
centigram
choreography
decagram
decigram
diagram
geography
gram
hectogram
ideogram
kilogram
milligram
monogram
parallelogram
photograph
pictogram
pictograph
telegram
telegraph

A list of words to print out for students can be found on the Digital Resource CD (filename: wordlists.pdf).

Teacher Background Information and Tips

Base *graph-*, *gram-* = "write," "draw"

In general vocabulary, the Greek base *graph-*, *gram-* means "write," "draw." It generates such familiar words as *biography* (a "written" life story), *geography* (discipline of "drawing" maps of Earth), and *photograph* (a picture produced or "drawn" by light).

In math, the base *gram* refers specifically to a "drawn" line. The word *parallelogram* provides a good example of this meaning of *gram*. A *parallelogram* is a quadrilateral with two pairs of parallel "drawn" lines. Similarly, a *diagram* is a figure consisting of "drawn lines."

Within the terminology of the metric system, the base *gram* has the specialized meaning of "gram," the basic unit of mass, or dry weight. The term *gram* for measurement of weight derives from the practice of "writing" or "drawing" a tiny mark etched on a scale. Scientists referred to that mark as a "gramma," which in Greek means "written thing." In this manner, the tiny etch mark written on a scale came to symbolize a small and precise unit of weight measurement.

Name: _____ Date: _____

About the Root:
Write About It

· ·

Directions: Read the information. Then answer the questions.

In general vocabulary, the Greek base *graph-, gram-* means "write" or "draw." In math, the base *gram* refers specifically to a "drawn" line. In the metric system, the base *gram* has another meaning. A *gram* is the basic unit of mass, or dry weight. *Gram* is a word by itself. It also is part of other words relating to dry weight (e.g., *kilogram, centigram*). The word *gram* has an interesting etymology. When scientists would measure items on a scale, they would make a notch on a scale to indicate the precise weight. These little jottings resembled tiny lines, and they were called *grams,* meaning "jot marks."

◎ What weighs more, a *decigram* or a *decagram*? How do you know?

_____

_____

Name: _____ Date: _____

About the Root:
Pictograms

Directions: Read the passage. Then answer the question.

> Imagine a road sign. It has an arrow with a right angle pointing left. It has a red circle around it with a slanted line through its diameter. What does this sign mean? It means "No left turn," all around the world. This is a *pictogram*, sometimes called an ideogram. It's a way of communicating meaning without using letters or words.
>
> Since ancient times, people have used pictograms to communicate. Some prehistoric cave drawings used pictograms. Pictograms are also the basis for cuneiforms and hieroglyphics, two ancient forms of writing.
>
> In math, pictograms can be used to show data. In this case, you would select images or symbolic figures to represent things or numbers of things. Suppose you wanted to graph the number of birds coming to a feeder by the hour. You could use a sketch of a bird to equal 10 birds. Then your *pictograph*, a graph using pictograms, would have hours on one axis and birds or fractions of birds on the other. Pictographs are not as precise as other forms of data graphing, but they are fun to look at!

◎ Sally saw 10 birds at her feeder at 7 A.M. At 10 A.M., she saw 5 birds. At 4 P.M., she saw 23 birds. Make a pictograph that displays Sally's data. (**Note:** You can use any symbol. Be sure to indicate if the symbol will stand for more than one bird.)

Name: _____ Date: _____

About the Root:
Measuring Solids

Directions: Read the passage. Then answer the question.

A song from the musical *Guys and Dolls* begins "I love you a bushel and a peck...." This is a strange way of saying, "I love you a lot." A bushel is a dry measurement that equals four pecks. A peck, also a dry measurement, equals two gallons. So, how much does the person singing the song love the other person? Eight gallons?

Besides bushels and pecks, the volume of dry goods is measured in other ways. Quarts and gallons are used for both solids and liquids, as are teaspoons and tablespoons. The volume of bulk goods is measured by filling standard-size containers. Containers and units often have the same name. A pint container holds a pint of strawberries, for example.

Solids can also be weighed. Here, especially for non-liquid ingredients in cooking and grocery shopping, the *gram* is the most important unit. A gram weighs about as much as a small paper clip. If you have ever looked at the nutritional information on the side of a food container, you have probably seen vitamin, mineral, and fat content listed as grams or as per gram.

Grams also form the basis of metric mass or weight. Prefixes added to -*gram* denote heavier or lighter weights. For example, a kilogram (about 2.2 pounds) is 1,000 grams. A milligram is $\frac{1}{1,000}$ of a gram.

◎ Gracie weighs 66 pounds. How many kilograms does she weigh? (**Hint:** Divide Gracie's weight in pounds by the number of pounds it takes to make a kilogram.)

_____

Name: _____ Date: _____

Divide and Conquer:
Words Associated with Writing

Directions: Use the Base/Prefix/Suffix Bank to help you identify the roots of the words below. Write the letter from the Definition Bank for the correct word.

Base/Prefix/Suffix Bank

dia- = "through," "across"   *mono-* = "one," "single"   *cart-* = "map"

Definition Bank

A. weight of $\frac{1}{1,000}$ gram

B. the science of map-making

C. a figure drawn in outline form

D. weight of 10 grams

E. a single letter or initial

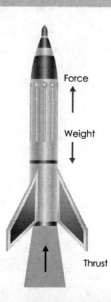

Word	First Base/Prefix Means	Second Base/Suffix Means	Definition
1. diagram			
2. cartography			
3. monogram			
4. decagram			
5. milligram			

Name: _____   Date: _____

Making Connections:
Equivalents

Directions: Match each numerical term or number in the first column with its equivalent in the second column.

Numerical Term/Number	Equivalent
_____ 1. 10 grams	**A.** 1 decigram
_____ 2. 0.1 gram	**B.** 0.02 gram
_____ 3. 2 milligrams	**C.** 1 decagram
_____ 4. 2 centigrams	**D.** 2 kilograms
_____ 5. 20 hectograms	**E.** 0.002 gram
_____ 6. 0.5 kilogram	**F.** 1 centigram
_____ 7. 0.01 gram	**G.** 1 hectogram
_____ 8. 5,000 grams	**H.** 5 hectograms
_____ 9. 100 grams	**I.** 5 kilograms
_____ 10. 500 grams	**J.** 0.5 kilogram

11. Are 500 *kilograms* heavier or lighter than 500 *milligrams*? How can you tell?

_____

_____

Base *liter-*

liter- = "liter," "liquid measurement"

Standards

Uses conventions of spelling in written compositions

Determines the meaning of words and phrases as they are used in a text, including figurative, connotative, and technical meanings

Materials

- *About the Root: Liters* (page 174)

- *About the Root: Measuring Liquids* (page 175)

- *About the Root: Cooking with the Metric System* (page 176)

- *Divide and Conquer: Words Associated with Liquid Measurement* (page 177)

- *Making Connections: Root Bank* (page 178)

Teacher Preparation

- Read and review the background information about the base *liter-* on page 173 to familiarize yourself with words associated with "liquid measurement."

- Read and review the glossary of the base found on the Digital Resource CD (filename: rootsglossary.pdf) for additional support.

Guided Practice

About the Root

1. Distribute copies of pages 174, 175, and/or 176 to students.

2. Tell students that *liter-* means "liter," which is a liquid measure. Students can read the passages and answer the questions independently or with partners. When they have concluded, invite sharing.

Divide and Conquer

3. Distribute copies of *Divide and Conquer: Words Associated with Liquid Measurement* (page 177). As you guide students through the activity page, use questions like these to generate discussion about each of the words:

   - Where is the meaning of "liter" or "liquid measurement" in the word _____?

   - How do you know _____ is a liquid measure?

   - Where might you see the word _____?

   - Can you think of an example of _____?

Base liter- *(cont.)*

Making Connections

4. Distribute copies of *Making Connections: Root Bank* (page 178).

5. Students can work independently or with partners.

6. To conclude, invite sharing. You might ask students to explain their math problems to partners. For example, ask several students to write their problems on the board so others can compare them.

Metric system words with liter-

centiliter

decaliter

deciliter

hectoliter

kiloliter

liter

milliliters

A list of words to print out for students can be found on the Digital Resource CD (filename: wordlists.pdf).

Teacher Background Information and Tips

Base *liter-* = "liter," "liquid measurement"

Ever since antiquity, the Greek base *liter-* has been associated with the measurement of liquids. (**Note:** This Greek base should not be confused with the Latin base *liter-*, which means "letter," as in *literal, alliteration,* and *literature.*) In ancient Greek, the word *litra* refers to a coin of either silver or gold, both of which are easily melted metals. Silver and gold coins could be melted and recast, and their value was determined by their weight.

The metric system retains this close association between the base *liter-* and liquid measurement. Specifically, the term *liter* is the weight of one kilogram of water.

As with the other units of measurement in the metric system (meters and grams), the base *liter* attaches to Latin numerical bases (*dec[i]-, cent[i]-, mill[i]-*) for fractional amounts of $\frac{1}{10}$, $\frac{1}{100}$, and $\frac{1}{1,000}$ of a liter. It also attaches to the Greek numerical bases (*deca-, hect[o]-, kil[o]-*) for multiple amounts of 10, 100, and 1,000 liters.

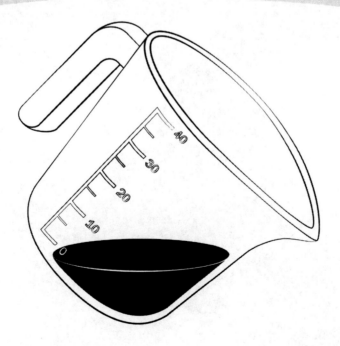

Name: _____ Date: _____

About the Root:
Liters

. . . .

Directions: Read the information. Then answer the question.

Ever since antiquity, the Greek base *liter-* has been associated with the measurement of liquids. In ancient Greek, a *litra* was a coin of either silver or gold. Silver and gold coins could easily be melted and recast, so their weight determined their value.

Today, in metric measurement, *liter* is used to measure liquids. Specifically, it is the weight of one kilogram of water. *Liter* can be used by itself, as in a two-liter bottle of soda pop. It can also be added to other bases (e.g., *deciliter, kiloliter*).

◎ Which contains more liquid, a deciliter or a kiloliter? How do you know?

_____

_____

_____

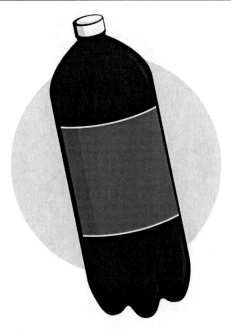

Name: _____ Date: _____

About the Root:
Measuring Liquids

Directions: Read the passage. Then answer the question.

Pints, quarts, gallons, liters, cubic meters, cubic centimeters...measuring liquids can be confusing! This is especially true in the United States or the United Kingdom, where both types of measures, metric and nonmetric, are used.

Even within the metric system, we have several ways to measure the volume of liquids. The most common may be the *liter* (spelled *litre* outside the United States). One liter of liquid has the mass or weight of almost exactly 1 kilogram. Another way to think about a liter is to imagine a 10-centimeter cube. The volume of this cube is a liter. A liter is also almost a liquid quart. Here's a little poem to help you remember this: "A liter of water is a pint and three quarter(s)."

Liters are usually used to measure liquids or solids that can be poured, such as sand or dry rice. How quickly something flows, like a river, is measured in liters per time unit (per hour, per day, etc.). But very large volumes, such as the amount of water needed to fill a swimming pool, are sometimes measured in cubic meters. And the amount of medicine you receive in an inoculation, for example, might be measured in cubic centimeters (cc). Measuring liquids can be confusing!

◎ Does it make sense to you that so many terms are used for measuring liquids? Why?

_____

_____

_____

_____

Name: _____ Date: _____

About the Root:
Cooking with the Metric System

Directions: Read the passage. Then answer the question.

To cook using metric measures, we first need to know the basic units and common prefixes. These are explained in the passage on page 175. Temperature must also be considered. The Celsius (or centigrade) scale is associated with metric measurement. In this scale, water freezes at 0° and boils at 100°. A hot oven is 200°. It's easy to find converters online to move from Fahrenheit to Celsius, or back and forth.

Converting other measurements for cooking is also easy. Most glass measuring cups have metric measures on one side. This helps for measuring liquids using liters or fractions of liters. Likewise, most kitchen thermometers are scaled to both Fahrenheit and Celsius readings. These are useful for cooking meat or candy. American measuring spoons can even be used to cook with the metric system. A teaspoon is about 5 milliliters, and a tablespoon is about 15 milliliters.

To cook using the metric system, you need to know the units of measure and the prefixes commonly attached to them. You also need to be able to convert temperatures and either convert or read metric scales on common cooking tools. It's not as hard as it seems!

A liter is the weight of one kilogram of water, about 2.2 pounds.

◎ Why would a person want or need to cook using the metric system?

_____

_____

_____

Name: _____   Date: _____

Divide and Conquer:
Words Associated with Liquid Measurement

Directions: By now you already know the roots that make up the words below. See how good your memory is! Write the letter from the Definition Bank for the correct word.

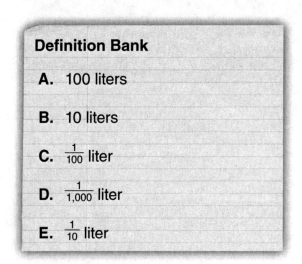

Definition Bank

A. 100 liters

B. 10 liters

C. $\frac{1}{100}$ liter

D. $\frac{1}{1,000}$ liter

E. $\frac{1}{10}$ liter

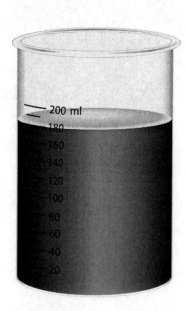

Word	First Base/Prefix Means	Second Base/Suffix Means	Definition
1. centiliter			
2. milliliter			
3. hectoliter			
4. decaliter			
5. deciliter			

Name: _____   Date: _____

Making Connections:
Root Bank

· ·

Directions: Use the Root Bank below to help you answer the questions. Either explain your reasoning or show your work.

Root Bank

$cent(i)\text{-} = \frac{1}{100}$ $hect(o)\text{-} = 100$ $mill(i)\text{-} = \frac{1}{1,000}$

$deca\text{-} = 10$ $kil(o)\text{-} = 1000$

1. How many liters are in a decaliter? _____

2. How would you change kiloliters to liters? _____

3. How would you change liters to kiloliters? _____

4. How many decaliters are in 5 liters? _____

5. 0.003 liters is how many milliliters? _____

6. 250 liters is how many hectoliters? _____

7. How many liters are in a kiloliter? _____

8. Are 500 *milliliters* more or less volume than 5 *kiloliters*? How can you tell?

   _____

   _____

9. Put these in order, from least volume to most volume: centiliter, decaliter, deciliter, hectoliter, kiloliter, liter, milliliter.

   _____

   _____

   _____

   _____

   _____

Answer Key

Unit I: Lesson 1–Numerical Bases/Prefixes: *cent(i)-* and *mill(i)-*

About the Root: Century and Millennium (page 22)

1. 100 years; Answers will vary.
2. 1,000 years; Answers will vary.

About the Root: Centigrade (page 23)

Answers will vary.

About the Root: SI Symbols (page 24)

Answers will vary

Divide and Conquer: Words Associated with 100 and 1,000 (page 25)

1. D
2. E
3. B
4. C
5. A

Making Connections: Numerical Equivalents (page 26)

1. F
2. H
3. D
4. A
5. B
6. C
7. E
8. G
9. I
10. J
11a. $2,500,000.00
11b. 3.5%

Unit I: Lesson 2– Prefixes *poly-* and *multi-*

About the Root Activities (pages 30–32)

Answers will vary on all three activities.

Divide and Conquer: Words Associated with Many (page 33)

1. B
2. D
3. E
4. C
5. A

Making Connections: Who/What Are We? (page 34)

1. C
2. E
3. D
4. B
5. A
6. F
7. G
8. H
9. Answers will vary.

Unit I: Lesson 3– Bases *integer-*, *integr-* and *frag-*, *fract-*

About the Root Activities (pages 38–40)

Answers will vary on all three activities.

Divide and Conquer: Words Associated with Whole and Broken (page 41)

1. D
2. E
3. B
4. A
5. C

Answer Key (cont.)

Making Connections: Magic Square (page 42)

A. 2		**F.** 4	
B. 7		**G.** 10	
C. 9		**H.** 3	
D. 6		**I.** 5	
E. 8		**J.** 1	

Magic Number = 18

Unit I: Lesson 4– Base *fin-, finit-*

About the Root Activities (pages 46–48)

Answers will vary on all three activities.

Divide and Conquer: Words Associated with End, Term, or Limit (page 49)

1. B
2. D
3. C
4. E
5. A

Making Connections: Fill in the Blank (page 50)

1. finite
2. infinitely
3. definitions
4. infinite
5. ad infinitum
6. confined
7. infinity
8. final
9. Answers will vary.
10. Answers will vary.

Unit I: Lesson 5– Base *vers-, vert-*

About the Root: Turning and Changing in Math (page 54)

3, 2, 1; Answers will vary.

About the Root: Transversals (page 55)

12; Sketches will vary.

About the Root: Converting Decimals, Percentages, and Fractions (page 56)

Answers will vary.

Divide and Conquer: Words Associated with Change (page 57)

1. F
2. A
3. C
4. B
5. E
6. D

Making Connections: Crossword Puzzle (page 58)

Across

4. triangle
6. direct
8. conversion
9. transversal
10. square

Down

1. vertical
2. inverse
3. perpendicular
5. vertex
7. angles

Answer Key *(cont.)*

Unit II: Lesson 1–Bases *gon-* and *angl-, angul-*

About the Root Activities (pages 62–64)
Answers will vary on all three activities.

Divide and Conquer: Words Associated with Angle and Corner (page 65)
1. C
2. E
3. A
4. D
5. B

Making Connections: Riddles (page 66)
Answers will vary.

Unit II: Lesson 2– Base *later-*

About the Root: Side to Side (page 70)
to the side of the quarterback; 4; triangle.

About the Root: Let's Go Fly a Kite! (page 71)
Answers will vary.

About the Root: Polygons and Quadrilaterals (page 72)
polygon, quadrilateral/quadrangle, parallelogram, rectangle, square

Divide and Conquer: Words Associated with Sides (page 73)
1. B
2. E
3. A
4. D
5. C

Making Connections: Name that Quadrilateral! (page 74)
1. A
2. D
3. E
4. C
5. B
6. One pair of opposite sides of the parallelogram should be marked with a single tic; the other pair of opposite sides should be marked with a double tic.
7. Another word for "trilateral polygon" is triangle.

Unit II: Lesson 3– Base *seg-, sec-, sect-*

About the Root Activities (pages 78–80)
Answers will vary on all three activities.

Divide and Conquer: Words Associated with Cutting (page 81)
1. B
2. D
3. E
4. C
5. A

Making Connections: Fill in the Blank (page 82)
1. intersection
2. sections
3. trisect
4. segment
5. sector
6. insects
7. intersect
8. bisected
9. dissecting
10. section
11. 3 angles of 30 degrees each.

Answer Key (cont.)

Unit II: Lesson 4– Bases *iso-* and *equ(i)-*, *equat-*

About the Root activities (pages 86–88)

Answers will vary on all three activities.

Divide and Conquer: Words Associated with Equality (page 89)

1. C
2. E
3. A
4. D
5. B

Making Connections: Fill in the Blank (page 90)

1. equinox
2. equilateral
3. isosceles
4. equiangular
5. equivalent
6. equation
7. isometric
8. equal
9. equidistant
10. Answers will vary.

Unit II: Lesson 5– Base *tang-*, *tag-*, *tig-*, *tact-*

About the Root activities (pages 94–96)

Answers will vary on all three activities.

Divide and Conquer: Words Associated with Touch (page 97)

1. D
2. A
3. E
4. C
5. B

Making Connections: Magic Square (page 98)

A. 10		**F.** 13	
B. 8		**G.** 12	
C. 6		**H.** 7	
D. 2		**I.** 5	
E. 9			

Magic Number = 24

Unit III: Lesson 1– Prefixes *peri-* and *circum-*

About the Root Activities (pages 102–104)

Answers will vary on all three activities.

Divide and Conquer: Words Associated with Around (page 105)

1. C
2. E
3. A
4. B
5. D

Making Connections: Who/What Am I? (page 106)

1. J
2. F
3. D
4. H
5. E
6. C
7. G
8. A
9. I
10. B
11. Answers will Vary.

Answer Key *(cont.)*

Unit III: Lesson 2– Prefixes *dia-* and *per-*

About the Root Activities (pages 110–112)
Answers will vary on all three activities.

Divide and Conquer: Words Associated with Through, Across, or Thorough (page 113)

1. E
2. A
3. C
4. B
5. D

Making Connections: Unscramble (page 114)

1. diametrically opposed
2. diameter
3. dialect
4. diagnostic tests
5. diagram
6. diagnose
7. dialogue
8. perpendicular
9. percent
10. per household
11. Answers will vary.

Unit III: Lesson 3– Prefixes *syn-, sym-, syl-* and *co-, con-, com-*

About the Root Activities (pages 118–120)
Answers will vary on all three activities.

Divide and Conquer: Words Associated with Togetherness (page 121)

1. C
2. E
3. A
4. B
5. D

Making Connections: Fill in the Blank (page 122)

1. congruent
2. concentric
3. contiguous
4. synchronize
5. coordinates
6. combination
7. syllables
8. converge
9. compound
10. conversion
11. Answers will vary.

Unit III: Lesson 4– Prefixes *hypo-* and *sub-*

About the Root (pages 126–128)
Answers will vary on all three activities.

Divide and Conquer: Words Associated with Below or Under (page 129)

1. B
2. D
3. E
4. C
5. A

Making Connections: Fill in the Blank (page 130)

1. submultiple
2. subset
3. hypothesis
4. hypothermia
5. hypotenuse
6. hypoglycemic
7. subdivide
8. hypodermic
9. subtotal
10. substandard
11. Answers will vary.

Answer Key *(cont.)*

Unit III: Lesson 5– Prefixes *hyper-* and *super-*, *sur-*

About the Root Activities (pages 134–136)
Answers will vary on all three activities.

Divide and Conquer: Words Associated with Over or Above (page 137)
1. D
2. B
3. E
4. C
5. A

Making Connections: Who/What Am I? (page 138)
1. G
2. F
3. H
4. B
5. E
6. C
7. D
8. A
9. I
10. J
11. Answers will vary.

Unit IV: Lesson 1– Base m*eter-*, metr-

About the Root: Measure Up (page 142)
Answers will vary.

About the Root: How Did Geometry Get Its Name? (page 143)
Answers will vary.

About the Root: Counting Steps (page 144)
Answers will vary, but should address the following: alike–both measure, both have to do with steps; different–using steps as unit of measurement vs. counting steps

Divide and Conquer: Words Associated with Measuring (page 145)
1. D
2. B
3. A
4. E
5. C

Making Connections: I Count! (page 146)
1. F
2. D
3. C
4. A
5. I
6. B
7. H
8. E
9. J
10. G
11. A *photometer* measures light, because the Greek base *photo(o)-* means "light."

About the Root: Latin Metric Terminology (page 150)
- $\frac{1}{100}$; 100
- $\frac{1}{1,000}$; 1,000

Answer Key (cont.)

Unit IV: Lesson 2– Numerical Bases *dec(i)-*, *cent(i)-*, and *mill(i)-*

About the Root: Metric System—The Basics (page 151)

Answers will vary.

About the Root: December (page 152)

Answers will vary.

Divide and Conquer: Latin Words Associated with Ten, Hundred, and Thousand (page 153)

1. A
2. C
3. B
4. D
5. E

Making Connections: Equivalents (page 154)

1. F
2. A
3. G
4. D
5. J
6. B
7. H
8. E
9. C
10. I
11. longer; Answers will vary.

Unit IV: Lesson 3– Numerical Bases *deca-*, *hect(o)-*, and *kil(o)-*

About the Root: Greek Metric Terminology (page 158)

- 10
- 1,000
- kilometer; Answers will vary.

About the Root: Decathlons (page 159)

Answers will vary.

About the Root: Megabytes and Gigabytes (page 160)

Answers will vary.

Divide and Conquer: Greek Words Associated with Ten, Hundred, and Thousand (page 161)

1. E
2. C
3. A
4. B
5. D

Making Connections: Magic Square (page 162)

A. 9
B. 2
C. 7
D. 4
E. 6
F. 8
G. 5
H. 10
I. 3
J. 1

Magic Number: 18

A kilometer is longer than a hectometer, because 1,000 is a larger quantity than 100.

Answer Key (cont.)

Unit IV: Lesson 4– Base *graph-, gram-*

About the Root: Write About It (page 166)

decagram; Answers will vary.

About the Root: Pictograms (page 167)

Answers will vary.

About the Root: Measuring Solids (page 168)

about 30 kilograms

Divide and Conquer: Words Associated with Writing (page 169)

1. C
2. B
3. E
4. D
5. A

Making Connections: Equivalents (page 170)

1. C
2. A
3. E
4. B
5. D
6. H
7. F
8. I
9. G
10. J
11. heavier; Answers will vary.

Unit IV: Lesson 5– Base *liter-*

About the Root: Liters (page 174)

kiloliter; Answers will vary.

About the Root: Measuring Liquids (page 175)

Answers will vary.

About the Root: Cooking with the Metric System (page 176)

Answers will vary.

Divide and Conquer: Words Associated with Liquid Measurement (page 177)

1. C
2. D
3. A
4. B
5. E

Making Connections: Root Bank (page 178)

1. 10
2. Multiply by 1,000
3. Divide by 1,000
4. 0.5
5. 3
6. 2.5
7. 1,000
8. less; Answers will vary.
9. milliliter, centiliter, deciliter, liter, decaliter, hectoliter, kiloliter

References Cited

ACT, Inc. *Reading Between the Lines: What the ACT Reveals About College Readiness in Reading.* Iowa City, IA: Author, 2006.

Baumann, James, Elizabeth C. Carr-Edwards, George Font, Cathleen A. Tereshinski, Edward J. Kame'enui, and Stephen Olejnik. "Teaching Morphemic and Contextual Analysis to Fifth-Grade Students." *Reading Research Quarterly* 37 (2002): 150–176.

Baumann, James F., George Font, Elizabeth C. Edwards, and Eileen Boland. "Strategies for Teaching Middle-Grade Students to Use Word-Part and Context Clues to Expand Reading Vocabulary." In *Teaching and Learning Vocabulary: Bringing Research to Practice*, edited by Elfrieda H. Hiebert and Michael L. Kamil, 179–205. Mahwah, NJ: Erlbaum, 2005.

Bear, Donald, Marcia Invernizzi, Shane Templeton, and Francine R. Johnston. *Words Their Way (5th Edition).* Upper Saddle River, NJ: Prentice Hall, 2011.

Beck, Isabel L., Margaret G. McKeown, and Linda Kucan. *Bringing Words to Life: Robust Vocabulary Instruction.* New York: Guilford, 2002.

Beck, Isabel, Charles A. Perfetti, and Margaret G. McKeown. "Effects of Long-Term Vocabulary Instruction on Lexical Access and Reading Comprehension." *Journal of Educational Psychology* 74 (1982): 506–521.

Biemiller, Andrew. "Implications for Choosing Words for Primary Grade Vocabulary." In *Teaching and Learning Vocabulary: Bringing Research to Practice*, edited by by Elfrieda H. Hiebert and Michael L. Kamil, 223–242. Mahwah, NJ: Erlbaum, 2005.

Biemiller, Andrew, and Naomi Slonim. "Estimating Root Word Vocabulary Growth in Normative and Advantaged Populations: Evidence for a Common Sequence of Vocabulary Acquisition." *Journal of Educational Psychology* 93 (2001): 498–520.

Blachowicz, Camille, and Peter Fisher. *Teaching Vocabulary in All Classrooms (3rd Edition).* Upper Saddle River, NJ: Pearson/Merrill/Prentice Hall, 2006.

Blachowicz, Camille, Peter Fisher, Donna Ogle, and Susan Watts-Taffe. "Vocabulary: Questions from the Classroom." *Reading Research Quarterly* 41 (2006): 524–538.

Carlisle, Joanne F. "Awareness of the Structure and Meaning of Morphologically Complex Words: Impact on Reading." *Reading and Writing: An Interdisciplinary Journal* 12 (2000): 169–190.

———. "Effects of Instruction in Morphological Awareness on Literacy Achievement: An Integrative Review." *Reading Research Quarterly* 45 (2010): 464–487.

Chandler, Richard E., and Kessel Schwartz. *A New History of Spanish Literature.* Baton Rouge, LA: LSU Press, 1961/1991.

Cunningham, Patricia M. *Phonics They Use: Words for Reading and Writing.* New York: Longman, 2004.

References Cited (cont.)

Graves, M.F., and S.M. Watts-Taffe. "The Place of Word Consciousness in a Research-Based Vocabulary Program." In *What Research Has to Say About Reading Instruction*, edited by Alan E. Farstrup and S. Jay Samuels, 140–165. Newark, DE: International Reading Association, 2002.

Harmon, Janis M., Wanda B. Hedrick, and Karen D. Wood. "Research on Vocabulary Instruction in the Content Areas: Implications for Struggling Readers." *Reading & Writing Quarterly* 21 (2005): 261–280.

Kame'enui, Edward J., Douglas W. Carnine, and Roger Freschi. "Effects of Text Construction and Instructional Procedures for Teaching Word Meanings on Comprehension and Recall." *Reading Research Quarterly* 17 (1982): 367–388.

Kieffer, Michael, and Nonie K. Lesaux. "Breaking Down Words to Build Meaning: Morphology, Vocabulary, and Reading Comprehension in the Urban Classroom." *The Reading Teacher* 61 (2007): 134–144.

LaFleur, Richard A. "Latin Students Score High On SAT and Achievement Tests." Classical Journal, 76 (3), 254. 1981.

Lehr, Fran, Jean Osborn, and Elfrieda H. Hiebert. "Research-Based Practices in Early Reading Series: A Focus on Vocabulary." 2004. http://eric.ed.gov/?id=ED483190

Mountain, Lee. "ROOTing Out Meaning: More Morphemic Analysis for Primary Pupils." *The Reading Teacher* 58 (2005): 742–749.

Nagy, William, Richard C. Anderson, Marlene Schommer, Judith Ann Scott, and Anne C. Stallman. "Morphological Families in the Internal Lexicon." *Reading Research Quarterly* 24 (1989): 262–282.

Nagy, William, and Judith Ann Scott. "Vocabulary Processes." In *Handbook of Reading Research, Vol. III*, edited by Michael L. Kamil, Peter B. Mosentahl, and P. David Pearson, and Rebecca Barr, 269–284. Mahwah, NJ: Erlbaum, 2000.

Porter-Collier, I.M. "Teaching Vocabulary Through the Roots Approach in order to Increase Comprehension and Metacognition." Unpublished masters degree project. Akron OH: University of Akron, 2010.

Rasinski, Timothy, and Nancy Padak. *From Phonics to Fluency (3rd Edition).* New York: Longman, 2013.

Rasinski, Timothy, Nancy Padak, Evangeline Newton, and Rick M. Newton. *Greek and Latin Roots: Keys to Building Vocabulary.* Huntington Beach, CA: Shell Educational Publishing, 2008.

Stahl, Steven A., and Marilyn M. Fairbanks. "The Effects of Vocabulary Instruction: A Model-Based Meta-Analysis." *Review of Educational Research* 56 (1986): 72–110.

Additional Practice Activities

Use the following activities to provide extra practice, to share with parents, or to differentiate instruction.

Be the Bard

Although most people recognize William Shakespeare as a great writer of plays and poetry, few realize that he was a great wordsmith. It has been estimated that Shakespeare invented approximately eight percent or one of every twelve unique words that he used. Many of these words were simply compounds made of already existing base words and/or affixes. Words such as *lackluster*, *premeditated*, and *noiseless* are but a few examples of the words he created. We think Shakespeare is a pretty good fellow to emulate. In *Be the Bard*, students create new words by using already learned roots. Student-invented words are put on display, and the inventor is asked to explain the meaning of his or her creation. Here are some words students invented: *automand* (an order that one gives to himself or herself), *terrameter* (a device for measuring land), and *contraduct* (to lead a group against another group). Although these created words are fanciful, students take genuine delight in using meaningful roots and affixes to create even more meaning.

Concentration (or Memory)

Select eight to ten words containing a root/base. Make double sets of word cards for each (or put the word and its definition on separate cards). Shuffle the cards and place them all facedown on a table. Players take turns trying to make matches. The player with the most matches wins the game.

Go Fish

Select four to six bases. For each, create a set of four words. Students use these to play "Go Fish."

Word War

Provide words containing the targeted base (or bases) written on cards. Play the card game "war" with them. Each player turns up a card. The person whose card a) comes first in alphabetical order, b) has more letters, or c) has more syllables wins the round, as long as he or she can say both words and their meanings. If the words are similar, players draw again, and the same rules apply. The player who wins this "war" takes all the cards. A player who gets all his or her partner's cards wins the game.

Additional Practice Activities *(cont.)*

List-Group-Label or Word Webs

Provide a base. Ask students to brainstorm words containing it. Write these on the board or chart paper. Then ask small groups to work with the words by:

◎ listing related terms and providing labels for them.

◎ developing a graphic, such as a web, that shows how the words are related.

◎ writing a summary text, using the grouping of words as an outline.

Root Word Riddles

Who doesn't enjoy solving a riddle? This strategy invites students to create and guess riddles with words from the same base. Give pairs of students a list of words that contain the targeted base. Each pair's job is to devise riddles for other students to solve. (You may want to model riddle creation for students.) See an example for *invisible* on the right.

Sketch to Stretch

Provide words written on slips of paper and distribute to students. Ask them to sketch something that reveals the word meaning. Then they share these with others to guess.

invisible

1. I have four syllables.

2. I have two word parts.

3. One part means "not."

4. The other means "see."

5. I mean not perceptible by the human eye.

What am I?

Twenty Questions

Students take turns asking questions that will help them figure out a "mystery" word that contains the targeted base. (If you and students keep a word wall of words containing the base, select words from it. Otherwise, you can list several words on the chalkboard.) They can ask up to 20 yes or no questions to try to determine the word.

Word Skits

List eight to ten words containing the targeted base on the board. Divide students into teams of three or four. Each team chooses one word and writes its definition on an index card. Working together, they create a skit that shows the meaning of the word. The skit is performed without words. Classmates try to guess the word being shown. Once the word is correctly identified, the definition is read out loud.

Additional Practice Activities *(cont.)*

Wordo

List twenty-four words containing the targeted base on the board. Duplicate a 4 x 4 or 5 x 5 Wordo Matrix for each student found on the Digital Resource CD (filenames: 4x4wordomatrix.pdf, 5x5wordomatrix.pdf). Ask students to choose a free box and mark it. Then have them write one of the words in each of the remaining boxes. Call a clue for each word: the definition, a synonym, an antonym, or a sentence with the target word deleted. Students figure out the correct target word, then put an *X* through it. (If you want to clear the sheets and play again, use small scraps of paper or other items to mark the squares.) When a student has *X*'s or markers in a row, column, diagonal, or four corners he or she can call out "Wordo!"

Word puzzles

Make crossword puzzles or word searches using http://www.puzzlemaker.com.

Word Sorts

Select about ten words containing the targeted root. Put the words on index cards. Provide one set of word cards to each pair of students. Ask students to group the words. Remind them that they will have to explain their groupings. Grouping may include:

◎ presence/absence of a prefix or suffix

◎ number of syllables

◎ presence/absence of a long vowel sound (in general, or a particular long vowel sound)

◎ words that refer to liquids and words that don't

◎ words that "cut" and words that don't

Invite students to tell about one of their groups, both the words contained in it and the reason for putting them together. Ask students to sort the same set of words in a different way. Each sort provides students another opportunity to think about both the words and their component parts.

Word Spokes

Duplicate a Word Spokes template for each student or pair of students found on the Digital Resource CD (filename: wordspokeschart.pdf). Put the targeted base or prefix on the board. Ask students to identify enough words containing the base to complete the chart. You may want to ask students to add sentences or illustrations of selected words, as well. Conclude the activity with sharing.

Contents of the Digital Resource CD

Student Resources		
Page	Title	Filename
22–26	Unit I Lesson 1—Numerical Bases/Prefixes *cent(i)-* and *mill(i)-*	centi_milli.pdf
30–34	Unit I Lesson 2—Prefixes *poly-* and *multi-*	poly_multi.pdf
38–42	Unit I Lesson 3—Bases *integer-, integr-* and *frag-, fract-*	integer_integr_frag_fract.pdf
46–50	Unit I Lesson 4—Base *fin-, finit-*	fin_finit.pdf
54–58	Unit I Lesson 5—Base *vers-, vert-*	vers_vert.pdf
62–66	Unit II Lesson 1—Bases *gon-* and *angl-, angul-*	gon_angl_angul.pdf
70–74	Unit II Lesson 2—Base *later-*	later.pdf
78–82	Unit II Lesson 3—Base *seg-, sec-, sect-*	seg_sec_sect.pdf
86–90	Unit II Lesson 4—Bases *iso-* and *equ(i)-, equat-*	iso_equi_equat.pdf
94–98	Unit II Lesson 5—Base *tang-, tag-, tig-, tact-*	tang_tag_tig_tact.pdf
102–106	Unit III Lesson 1—Prefixes *peri-* and *circum-*	peri_circum.pdf
110–114	Unit III Lesson 2—Prefixes *dia-* and *per-*	dia_per.pdf
118–122	Unit III Lesson 3—Prefixes *syn-, sym-, syl-* and *co-, con-, com-*	syn_sym_syl_co_con_com.pdf
126–130	Unit III Lesson 4—Prefixes *hypo-* and *sub-*	hypo_sub.pdf
134–138	Unit III Lesson 5—Prefixes *hyper-* and *super-, sur-*	hyper_super_sur.pdf
142–146	Unit IV Lesson 1—Base *meter-, metr-*	meter_metr.pdf
150–154	Unit IV Lesson 2—Numerical Bases *dec(i)-, cent(i)-,* and *mill(i)-*	deci_centi_milli.pdf
158–162	Unit IV Lesson 3—Numerical Bases *deca-, hect(o)-,* and *kil(o)-*	deca_hecto_kilo.pdf
166–170	Unit IV Lesson 4—Base *graph-, gram-*	graph_gram.pdf
174–178	Unit IV Lesson 5—Base *liter-*	liter.pdf

Teacher Resources		
Pages	Resource	Filename
16	Standards Chart	standards.pdf
NA	Functions of Prefixes and Suffixes	functions.pdf
NA	4 x 4 Wordo Matrix	4x4wordomatrix.pdf
NA	5 x 5 Wordo Matrix	5x5wordomatrix.pdf
NA	Word Spokes Chart	wordspokeschart.pdf
NA	Student Word Lists	wordlists.pdf
NA	Flashcards	flashcards.pdf
NA	Roots Glossary	rootsglossary.pdf